Julie Parker is one of Austr
body image and eating disord
social worker and life and bu
ages a full time counselling and coaching practice
specialising in supporting people with negative body
image and eating disorders, with a belief that recovery
is possible for everyone. Julie has appeared on
Sunrise, *The Morning Show* and *Lateline*, and in pub-
lications such as *Practical Parenting*, *Wellbeing* and
Cosmopolitan magazines. Julie lives in Melbourne
with her husband, step-daughter and feline therapeutic assistants; Cookie and Leo.

My Recovery

*Inspiring Stories, Recovery Tips and
Messages of Hope from Eating
Disorder Survivors*

Julie Parker

Momentum

First published by in 2012
This edition published in 2012 by Momentum
Pan Macmillan Australia Pty Ltd
1 Market Street, Sydney 2000

A CIP record for this book is available at the National Library of
Australia

My Recovery: Inspiring Stories, Recovery Tips and Messages of Hope
from Eating Disorder Survivors

EPUB format: 9781743340707
Mobi format: 9781743340721
Print on Demand format: 9781743340738

Cover design by XOU Creative

Copyedited by Kylie Mason

Proofread by Laura Cook

Macmillan Digital Australia: www.macmillandigital.com.au

To report a typographical error, please email
errors@momentumbooks.com.au

Visit www.momentumbooks.com.au to read more about all our books
and to buy books online. You will also find features, author interviews
and news of any author events.

*Dedicated to Claire Vickery for believing
all those with eating disorders have wings
and can fly free*

Table of Contents

Introduction

Recovery from an eating disorder is possible.

Even after suffering for many torturous years and through numerous hospitalisations, people triumph over eating disorders and become well. Even after depression, anxiety and having torturous feelings about food, self and body, healing begins. Even after resisting countless invading negative thoughts and low self-esteem, confidence and self-love is regained. Even after wanting life to end, the desire to live, and live well, takes hold.

The life and eating disorder experiences shared by the women and men within *My Recovery* are testament to this possibility. Each story is a personal journey of what it is like to live with anorexia nervosa, bulimia nervosa, binge eating disorder, an eating disorder not otherwise specified or a cruel combination. They reveal the true suffering and intricacy of what it means to have an eating disorder and contain real lessons, not only about the illness, but about life itself.

Eating disorders are illnesses we are still trying to understand in terms of prevention, onset and cure. These stories help us to enter the reality of how eating disorders develop, the triggers that make them worse, the behaviours that make them so devastating and, ultimately, the necessary means to recover from them. These stories are also myth busters, dispelling the falsehoods that accompany eating disorders, including that they are a lifestyle choice, that families are to blame for their onset and that those experiencing them are selfish and attention-seeking.

I wrote *My Recovery* in response to the countless times my therapeutic clients have asked to be put in touch with someone who has 'been there', someone who 'knows how I feel', someone who has 'survived and is well', someone who can 'show me how'. These requests have never come as surprise to me. Eating disorders are isolating and overwhelming illnesses that are still misunderstood by large sectors of the community and even by well-meaning loved ones. The desire to be able to talk to or learn from a real-life sur-vivor is therefore very strong and can be a powerful tool in recovery.

My Recovery was also inspired by the many surviv-ors of eating disorders I've met who had an intense desire to share their experiences in a way that could bring meaning and hope to others. They wanted to pass on how they beat their eating disorder to live free of its manipulation, degrading thoughts and punish-ing behaviours. They wanted to say, 'I did it! And you can do it too!'

My Recovery is chiefly a guide, a way to support those in recovery and those who care for and love them. My wish is for the messages of hope and the recovery tips to provide both encouragement and tan-gible strategies to assist in their journey. While not an academic or clinical text, I also believe that *My Recovery* can offer professionals working in the field of eating disorders a deeper insight into this illness, and infuse their own practice with wisdom and knowledge gained from those with direct experience of an eating disorder.

Writing *My Recovery* has been the most joyous, challenging, humbling and inspiring experience of my life. I am forever indebted to the courage shown by all the survivors in sharing a difficult chapter in their lives in such an open and gracious way. I knew some quite well and have been privileged to call them friend and colleague. Others I met for the first time when we sat in cafes, homes and gardens to share their stories and inspire others to never give up the belief that recovery is possible for all. Those times, and the times writing these stories, were filled with laughter, contemplation, learning and tears.

If you are holding this book in your hands and wondering if recovery is ever possible for you, I hope *My Recovery* shows that it *absolutely is.* May you find connection, comfort, inspiration and guidance in these pages and find your way back to your true self, knowing that you can and will be well. Every person who shared their story in *My Recovery* wished for me to tell you they believe in you. Their stories and recovery tips will show you why.

Julie Parker

Author's Note

The eighteen stories in *My Recovery* are real-life accounts of eating disorder journeys from onset through struggle to recovery. No parts of the stories have been fabricated; each is an entirely honest account. In some instances a name or names contained within the story have been changed for personal reasons.

Each story was written after an in-depth interview or interviews with each survivor and the majority of the words in their story are exactly their own.

There are no weights, measurements or in-depth detail of ritualistic behaviours in any of the survivors' stories in *My Recovery*. This is due to my and the survivors' wishes to be part of a book that focuses on the recovery aspect of eating disorder journeys, and for their stories not to be a potential trigger or afford someone the opportunity to compare their own experiences or things such as weight or calorie intake. I don't believe the omission of this information makes the stories any less powerful or meaningful, and in fact, I hope it allows the reader to focus more on the emotional and psychological pain that is the driving factor beneath these survival stories, rather than what survivors did or didn't eat or weigh.

The word *carer* or *carers* is used in places where you may usually see the word *parent*. This is because many children, young people and adults are being cared for by someone other than a parent, or in partnership with a parent, while they have an eating disorder. A carer may be a trusted adult, a sibling, a friend, or any person significantly involved in caring for someone in recovery from an eating disorder.

Key Reflections

The real-life stories in *My Recovery* clearly show that every person's eating disorder journey is an individual one. There are, however, many similar thought patterns, experiences and themes running through these stories, which those in recovery from an eating disorder, as well as carers and professionals, can learn from. These stories allow us to delve into eating disorders not from a text book or medical journal, but as they are experienced by those who had to endure and overcome them.

Some of the themes we can learn from include experiences within families and at school as well as behaviours and feelings such as dieting, low self-esteem, making comparisons and perfectionism. Each has the potential to teach us more about the lived eating disorder experience and how it can be caught early and supported by both carers and professionals alike.

Family

Eating disorders are complex mental illnesses that cannot and should not be blamed on any single thing, person or incident. Despite this, the family of a child or adult who is experiencing an eating disorder often has the blame placed on them for what their loved one is going through. This punitive approach helps no one – not the family and certainly not the child or person experiencing the eating disorder. It only serves to drive blame and shame further inwards at a time when a family must come together with more love and compassion than they might previously ever have had to muster.

These stories clearly show that there is no one type of family within which an eating disorder develops. Many of the storytellers come from very loving homes where they felt cared for and supported.

'I had a very blessed upbringing in Melbourne with loving parents.' Danni

'I love the fact that I come from a very close and loving Tassie family.' Elizabeth

Others describe difficult family upbringings such as emotional abuse, divorce and alcoholism, but in many cases state that the experience of having an eating disorder brought them closer as they faced the issue together.

'I never felt I belonged to a family unit.' Solveig

'Mum and I always clashed and would fight on a daily basis.' Jessica

These survivors came from families that are little different from yours or mine. Some have parents who have been happily married for many years; some come from blended families, others from broken ones. They are only children, eldest children, middle children, children with one sibling, and children with many siblings. Some describe having every material need catered for; others grew up in more humble circumstances. There are city girls, country girls and suburban guys. They come from families who are stable with no obvious pressing issues until the arrival of an eating disorder. They come from families struggling with everyday concerns and heartaches as well as triumphs. They come from families where mental illness and a lack of connection and affection are profoundly felt.

In other words, they are like all families.

Recovery Reflection

If you are caring for a loved one, child or adult, who has an eating disorder, or are concerned they may have one, you can play a significant role in their recovery. In fact, families can be – and are – a core component in eating disorder healing and are even seen as a vital part of an official treatment team. You should not blame yourself for the development of this illness in your loved one's life; this will only contribute to you turning on yourself or other family members. If you seek assistance from professionals and believe you are being 'pointed at' rather than encouraged with strategies and skills to assist, or not made to feel like you are part of your loved one's recovery team, it is your right to seek assistance elsewhere.

School

School plays a very significant role in the lives of many of these survivors in both positive and negative ways. While school has a large impact on nearly all of us, there are examples within these stories of school experiences that are deeply intertwined with the onset of an eating disorder. Many describe feeling anxious about school and, in particular, transitioning from primary to high school. They describe feeling lost and unsure with their peers, being afraid of not fitting in or already knowing they don't fit in.

'I felt sick about going into Year Seven.' Anna

'My anxiety increased when I started school.' Nikki

These descriptions are significant as we know that the development of anxious feelings about important things in our life can lead to introspection, comparisons to others and low self-esteem and confidence. At a time when a child or young person is trying to fit in with their peer group and find friends who allow them to have meaningful connections outside their family, such anxiety can be a difficult thing to cope with.

Other survivors express a great love for school, were highly academic and driven to achieve exceptional marks. While it is a positive thing that many enjoyed school and their studies, in some instances, the drive for perfect scores can lead to the need to be a perfect person. Such perfectionism can easily be a driving force behind placing untold pressure and expectations on themselves and the setting of standards that are not only unbalanced, but unattainable.

'As an absolute perfectionist, school work was extremely important to me.' Emma Kate

Further school experiences are described by survivors as being incredibly torturous and traumatic, usually as a result of bullying at the hands of other students. These experiences often involve systematic bullying over a period of months and even years. Bullying is described by many survivors as playing a pivotal role in the onset of their eating disorder due to the way their self-esteem and confidence plummeted. Others see it as an issue that worsened their illness.

'After such a prolonged period of teasing, my previously positive self-esteem was destroyed.' Kylie Rose

'I became the scapegoat of the group and they started to tease me and call me fat.' Mitchell

Recovery Reflection

These experiences teach us that carers need to be mindful of the transition period between primary and high school, which usually takes place at the onset of puberty. This uncertainty and anxiety, if left unchecked, can develop into higher level concerns relating to body image, self-acceptance and the potential development of an eating disorder. It is also important for carers to understand that there is such a thing as too much study. Any child or young person who does not value time away from their studies to do other enjoyable activities, or becomes upset if they do not achieve perfect marks, requires loving support to help them find better balance in their life.

It is important to take reports of bullying seriously. While there certainly are strategies that children and young adults can be taught to help them cope better with teasing and bullying, ultimately, schools should be bully-free zones, where all students can attend free of threat. All carers have a right to expect this and demand it, if necessary, of their loved one's educational institution.

Self-esteem

Either before or during their eating disorder journey, all of the survivors experienced significant self-esteem issues, including a lack of self-worth and belief in themselves. They describe feeling lost, unworthy and even frightened about who they were and their place in the world. This is often where the eating disorder took hold, or at the very least was made worse, enabling the disorder to thrive in a frail human host who found it difficult having the confidence to make even the smallest of decisions.

'I devastatingly felt I was not worthy of nourishment or of love.' Hannah

'It was almost as if I thought I wasn't good enough to be friends with certain people.' Laura

Recovery Reflection

Self-esteem is a key issue in the development of all eating disorders. It is not normal or acceptable for any person to consistently question who they are and where they fit in the world, or to hate themselves. This is not a feeling that any person should live with. It should also not be seen as something that is a normal part of 'teenage angst' or 'growing pains', but is actually a sign that a child or young person is struggling significantly to exist in their own skin and in need of loving support.

If your loved one is showing signs of having low self-esteem and is consistently putting themselves down, open up channels of communication by asking them how they feel, why they feel so down, what may be troubling them and how you can help. Offer a warm hug and a non-judgemental approach, including being open to them saying they are struggling and may require professional support.

Comparisons

A behaviour shared by many of the survivors is a tendency to compare themselves to others, both as a person as a whole, and with a focus on their body – weight, shape and appearance. Such comparisons can clearly be seen to give rise to feelings of inadequacy and an intensely negative train of thought. Comparing themself to others elicits the same negative results for a child or young person as it does for an adult.

The survivors believed themselves to be less attractive, less intelligent, less worthy or simply *less than* others around them. Survivors sometimes develop a false belief that they are less worthy of friendship, attention, support, help and love because they are not as 'good' as others. This mindset further fuels the grip that an eating disorder has, particularly through convincing the survivor that they are indeed all of the things they falsely believe about themselves and deserve to be experiencing such pain.

> 'There's no doubt I compared myself to other boys around me and I didn't feel as if I measured up well.' George

Recovery Reflection

Excessive comparison to others is a direct result of low self-esteem and a need to look outside of oneself for validation and reassurance. The result, however, is rarely, if ever, reassurance, but rather a plummeting of self-worth. This happens when a negative mindset grasps the perspective that those they are comparing themselves with are 'better'. This is never more the case than for those with an eating disorder, who are struggling with an internal dialogue that convinces them they are not as worthy or important as others.

In supporting someone with an eating disorder who regularly compares themselves to others, gentle encouragement to be concerned only with themselves and their own healing is a necessary and supportive behaviour. This can also be very helpful for those who are comparing their recovery journey to others' and potentially getting caught up in thoughts of others being 'better' or 'further along' or 'more stable' than they are, when none of these things may be accurately known. It is much better to have an inwards focus that recognises that all recovery journeys and paths are different and in many ways incomparable.

Puberty

Many of the survivors, particularly the female ones, describe having a very difficult time either just before or while going through puberty. This includes concerns with their period – such as not wanting it to come as it would signify leaving behind girlhood and the beginning of womanhood – and, in some instances, not even being told what a period was and what to expect when they got it.

Puberty can be a challenging time for any child, but these stories highlight that when unprepared or unaware of the changes taking place, especially if combined with an anxious mindset or low self-esteem, the impact on a child can be a negative and far-reaching one. For some, the unexpected weight gain during this stage of life is too much to cope with and can result in the onset of an eating disorder.

'Going through puberty, I struggled to acknowledge that I was changing and becoming a woman.'
Sophie

'When my body began to change I had no idea what was happening to me. No one had ever told me.' Kirsty

Our bodies are not static entities. They shift and grow and change daily and every person blessed to make it to adulthood will experience a significant amount of this change and growth. Just because puberty is a part of every person's life, however, does not make it an easy or trouble-free experience. For some children and young people it is a time of confusion, embarrassment and even fear.

These negative feelings can be greatly reduced or even eliminated entirely if carers are open about puberty and talk to children about all the necessary details of what is happening to them and their body in a way that does not signify it to be a secretive or embarrassing life event. This includes openly discussing what periods are and what happens when you get them, the growing of pubic hair and breasts, changes in genitalia and voice, and the normalcy of putting on weight and changes in body shape. When a child learns from the most trusted adults in their life that their body is beautiful, never wrong or unacceptable, it can have a profoundly positive impact on them and their body image and self-confidence for life. These stories highlight to us how important it is for adults to be open with children about puberty and all the changes they can expect to have happen to them.

Perfectionism

As mentioned previously, perfectionist tendencies run high in survivors: patterns of thinking and behaviour such as constantly striving, never resting, always pushing and wanting more of themselves are apparent. So in turn is exhaustion, introspection, rigidity and a constant desire to be exemplary and never let anyone down. In many instances, this thinking translates into a desire to be 'perfect' in body and appearance, hence the eating of only pure and 'good' foods, and to be as thin and attractive as possible. There are clear attempts by many of the survivors to try to control their body through what they were eating or not eating (their external world), while they were feeling lost, out of control and lacking in a sense of self (their internal world).

'I was an absolute perfectionist.' Laura

'My thinking was, "Why bother doing something if you didn't do it to your best?"' Elizabeth

Recovery Reflection

We are all perfectly imperfect as human beings. This is a fact we should embrace in ourselves and encourage others to embrace as well, recognising that it can be the nuances and differences in us that make us all so interesting and unique. There is no such thing as true perfection in a person, and even the belief there is can be dangerous. Believing that perfection is something that can be reached can be a catalyst for multiple destructive behaviours that then either lead into an eating disorder or worsen it. Populist culture also plays a role here, particularly through vehicles such as advertising, in repeatedly trying to sell the notion that you can attain a perfect body, skin, house and even life. This fantasy construct holds a great deal of power for many people and prompts a desire for something that is not only futile, but also may contribute to an ill mindset.

Embracing imperfection in ourselves and others is a forgiving, powerful and beautiful thing to do, especially if you are caring for or starting to notice that a loved one may be struggling with signs of low self-esteem, perfectionism or an eating disorder. Encouraging someone to relax rigid thought patterns, be gentle and kind to themselves and learn, not punish, when inevitable life mishaps and mistakes occur, can go a long way in supporting them to release the belief that they must be exemplary in every way.

Dieting

Starting a diet is clearly the beginning of the descent into an eating disorder for many of these survivors. The reasons given for going on a diet vary, but in nearly all cases it is underpinned by low self-esteem and being worried about their body's weight, shape or size. It is evident that once many started dieting they did not know when to stop, then how to stop, not realising they were hurtling into a serious mental illness.

What may have started out as a seemingly innocent attempt to 'better themselves', 'tone up' or 'feel more confident' took the survivors down a sinister path of loneliness and deprivation that saw their eating disorder get stronger.

'The second [modelling] agency told me I had to lose three kilograms, giving me instructions on what foods to cut from my diet.' Solveig

'My severe dieting was a subconscious attempt to try and both fit in and feel better about myself.' Sophie

Recovery Reflections

We are warned of the dangers of things such as excessive sun exposure and how it can translate into a life-threatening illness such as melanoma, but rarely of the danger and futility of dieting and the horrifying results it can inflict on someone's life. People do not fail diets, diets fail people. Sometimes this failure may be simply that they do not work (i.e., they don't result in long-term weight loss) or, as in the cases of these stories, that they are the catalyst for the development of the torturous relationship with food, body and self that comes with all eating disorders.

If you become aware that a loved one in your life is dieting, be mindful of what is really going on for them, underneath the surface of their desire to change their body. Are they feeling low in confidence and self-esteem? Are they excessively worried about their body? Do they feel as if there is something wrong with them and they must change to fit in or feel better? What are they possibly attempting to control through their eating that they cannot control in another area of their life? Gentle but supportive questioning that focuses on feelings rather than food and what they may be either eating or not eating, will help you to uncover the real source of distress for your loved one.

Unintentional Weight Loss

Many survivors state that when they first changed what they were eating they did not mean to lose weight, or lose a great deal of weight; it was just something that happened. This is something that can happen to any person who changes their diet, especially if combined with low self-esteem. This is a clear indication of the intensely seductive and negative power of diets and dieting behaviour and why, in some instances, the potential fallout of restrictive eating – whether in calories, food type, food groups, food combining or any other food 'rule' – can never be fully known.

The onset of an eating disorder mindset that may involve being driven to lose more weight, eat less food, exercise at greater intensity and engage in other means of self-punishment can take hold at any time. These stories show us the descent into this torturous illness was never intentional, never wanted, and certainly never deserved. Rather, it was something that by the time it had set in, the survivor was at a point where it was going to be a long road back to pre-dieting and pre-body-occupation days and happier times.

'I didn't have an intention to lose a lot of weight but it happened anyway.' Michelle

'Body image was never a factor for me and I certainly never felt a desire to lose weight.' Emma Kate

Recovery Reflection

No one can ever truly know what will happen to either their mind or body when they begin a diet. There may be an intention to lose a lot of weight and only a small amount of weight loss or none at all occur. There may be an intention to lose only a small amount of weight, or even just 'tone up', and the result may be, as can be seen in some of these survival stories, a great deal of weight loss.

When this weight loss happens, whether intentional or not, it often changes the mindset of not only how someone sees themselves but how they cognitively process the world around them – relationships, roles, achievements and more. While at some point along a survivor's weight-loss continuum they may have experienced a boost in self-confidence and belief, these stories show us how fleeting that time can be, as their mindset showed an inability to stop dieting and restricting and, in turn, their body continued to lose weight. This further shows us how vital it is to gently question and support someone we care for if we know they are dieting, being aware that at any point in time their mind and body may begin to betray them with firstly unintentional weight loss and then intentional weight loss coupled with the destructive force of an eating disorder mindset.

Validation and Comments

We live in a world that glamourises and values thinness and the reality of how this can affect someone is evident in a number of these stories. Many survivors received validation and praise from others when they first lost weight, which in turn spurred them on to lose more, even if such weight loss was clearly not only unnecessary but dangerous.

We must stop placing high value on things such as weight and weight loss and valuing people for external reasons. When we compliment someone about their weight loss we can never be certain if we are inadvertently contributing to a sick mindset. Some survivors were further tipped into their eating disorder – or at the least saw their self-esteem plummet – when others made a passing comment about their weight, shape or appearance.

'My weight loss attracted comments at school. Girls asked me how I was doing it and boys began to notice me.' Hannah

'After a comment from one of Mum's friends that I had "a bit of a double chin", I made a conscious decision to get rid of that "problem".' Anna

Recovery Reflection

While it is generous and positive to give someone a compliment, commenting on someone's weight loss, or indeed anything about their appearance, can be fraught with danger. Because of the strong societal construct that to be thin is good and to be fat is bad, it is common for people who have lost weight to be praised, supported and even revered. This validates not only the person losing weight, but weight-loss behaviour, often prompting a desire in someone to be even thinner than they are, based on the premise they are doing the good, the right and the *expected* thing. And they should keep going.

We need as a whole society to be aware not only that commenting on someone's weight loss can actually fuel an eating disorder mindset or illness but also that there are much more valuable things to praise each other for. Our character, intelligence, passions and the way we care for others and the wider community, just to name a few, should hold much greater importance when we contemplate the type of person we or others are.

Difficult Relationships

It is not surprising to learn that many of the survivors who share their stories in this book experienced difficult intimate relationships either before or during their eating disorder journey. Low self-esteem and lack of self-worth are the driving factors beneath these difficulties, as well as a distinct 'losing' of themselves in a relationship, potentially with a desire to validate and fill the negative spaces they had within themselves. The searching for love outside of oneself is strongly evident, but ultimately futile.

Relationships can be difficult to manage and maintain for even the most well and positive of people. They require commitment, communication, effort and self-reflection as well as the ability to give and receive affection and love. For any person experiencing the demeaning thoughts and behaviours that come with an eating disorder – and the negative mindset that discourages self-love and care – the demands of a relationship are extremely hard. This certainly did not stop some of the survivors from trying to enter or stay in a relationship, but the relationship became just one more issue to deal with in their recovery journey.

'I found myself entangled in a terrible relationship I didn't have the strength to get out of.' Kirsty

'I had sacrificed everything that was special and important to me to ensure I was something he wanted.' Michelle

Recovery Reflection

If you are in a relationship with someone you suspect or know has an eating disorder then whether you realise it or not, you are most likely to be that person's most significant recovery carer. You may already be aware of this and doing all you can to not only support them but also your relationship as a whole. If unaware, there are many positive things you can do to care for your loved one, with the recommended starting point being to ask them what they want, what they need, and how you can be there for them in a way that is meaningful and positive.

If you are aware that a loved one who has an eating disorder is in an unhealthy or destructive relationship, it can give rise to very frustrated and worried feelings

– you may feel powerless or not know what to do. Even though you may want to intervene or even insist they end the relationship, the best thing you can do is to focus on them rather than their partner and demonstrate how much you care for and love them. When someone knows this, it usually prompts greater feelings of trust and connection, which may then lead to them opening up to you about the relationship and how they might be able to better manage it.

Overexercising

Exercise is a positive, worthwhile and necessary thing for us to do for our health, but one that in today's world is often tied up with messages of weight loss. This connection can often drive people to overexercise or develop a difficult relationship with activity and movement rather than exercising simply for the fun and positive benefits it brings. A number of the survivors talk about how overexercising became an enormous problem for them while ill as a means to burn calories, lose weight and punish themselves. This is sometimes a less talked about and known aspect of eating disorders but is still a behaviour that is highly dangerous.

It is also important to note that someone who is unwell can hide overexercising under the guise of getting fit or being healthy. In fact, too much exercise can be a terrible symptom of an eating disorder and someone who is very unwell. Overexercising is also a behaviour that requires support and treatment as soon as possible for the physical complications it can promote in someone's body, which may range from stress fractures and shin splints, to severe dehydration and heart attack.

'I began to barely eat and would exercise furiously.' Faye

'By now I was obsessively running everywhere, even in my own bedroom, and I knew I needed a serious intervention.' Danni

Recovery Reflection

If you are feeling concerned that someone you care for may be overexercising or exercising in a way that is punitive, then your instinct is likely to be correct. There are varying levels of recommended exercise for children and adults and therefore what may be reasonable and OK for one person may not be for another, but exercising when injured or for hours on end, refusing to go a day without exercising, and exercising until exhaustion are unhealthy and dangerous behaviours for any person. They are a clear sign that your loved one is in need of caring intervention and assistance.

As always, the approach to assist should be done in a caring and gentle way that focuses on the underlying feelings your loved one will likely be grappling with rather than focusing on the exercise, which is just the outer manifestation of the pain they are experiencing.

Inner Voice

If your life has been touched by an eating disorder or you have studied or worked with people who have lived with an eating disorder, you will be aware that many people experiencing the illness describe hearing an intensely negative voice inside their head that often drowns out their own thoughts. This voice – sometimes called a 'negative head' – is a little known aspect of the illness among the wider community and therefore is often misunderstood, especially as it is something that cannot be seen with the naked eye. This horrible and berating inner voice is described by survivors as taking over their ability to think rationally, driving them to hurt themselves, cease eating and turn against their loved ones.

It is a powerful force reported by many, one that is steeped in making them believe they are worthless and not deserving of help. The voice is entirely the construct of an eating disorder and at the core of many survivors' experiences; it makes them turn away from formerly loved family members and friends and refuse help.

It is only through given love and self-love and professional help that sufferers can come to realise that the voice is not their true or healthy voice, but rather part of their illness. This makes the separation of themselves from the eating disorder voice vital in recovery, as is the carers' understanding that survivors' upsetting behaviours, words and feelings are caused by the dominating voice. Such behaviours are not what survivors want to do, it's the 'negative head' that has sucked their true personality and will away.

'At thirteen years of age I was completely under the control of rex and I did everything he said.' Elise

'I did have an anorexic voice that would tell me I was fat, needed to exercise more and that no one would hang out with me if I wasn't thin.' Mitchell

Recovery Reflection

One of the most powerful and healing things any person caring for someone with an eating disorder can do is be a part of helping them separate themselves from the illness they are experiencing. This means that when the eating disorder is driving the behaviour of a loved one through means such as lashing out, deception or refusal of food, help or love, they realise such behaviour is not usual for the person and is a result of them being sick with an eating disorder. While it can be very hard to take when standing in the presence of the person you love, getting angry or upset yourself can actually 'feed' the eating disorder and make it stronger.

What will tear the illness down and build your loved one up is not responding or engaging with what is clearly eating disorder communication and behaviour, but instead focusing on encouraging, nurturing and loving the lost and frightened person in front of you.

Multiple Eating Disorders and Dual Diagnosis

A significant number of survivors have experienced more than one type of eating disorder, often transitioning from one to another at different times along their recovery journey. A number of survivors move from the fasting and restriction that comes with anorexia, to the extreme consumption of food that comes with a binge eating disorder. Such transitioning shows the complexity of eating disorders and highlights the fact that these are illnesses that have their roots not in someone's relationship to food, but rather the negative feelings and thought patterns that underpin that behaviour. It also teaches us that every stage of someone's eating disorder can be very dangerous and just because someone may have gained weight due to a change in the way they are eating, does not mean they are not unwell and in need of professional help.

'I was constantly dieting, bingeing and starving.'
Laura

'Despite stopping purging, I instead decided to simply eat foods with no fat in them.' Ally

These survivors' stories also teach us that eating disorders are often accompanied by other mental illnesses, making their treatment and recovery harder and more complex. Diagnoses of depression, anxiety, self-harming, obsessive compulsive disorder, post-traumatic stress disorder and bipolar disorder are all present in a number of these journeys. While this clearly makes recovery a more complicated process and one that requires specialist help, it also shows the depth of courage and fortitude many have in overcoming not just one or two but even three different types of mental illness.

'I didn't want to deal with another diagnosis and I gave up for a while as I thought now that even if I recovered from the eating disorder it wouldn't matter, as I would always have the bipolar.' Nikki

'I developed major depression. It was such a horrible experience; one I wouldn't wish on anyone.' Elise

Recovery Reflections

The onset and existence of an eating disorder can co-exist with and hide other illnesses such as depression, anxiety or addiction, making them harder to detect and treat. Seeing a loved one as a whole person makes all aspects of their wellbeing a priority and as important to care for and treat as any other.

If you are caring for someone who has an eating disorder and either suspect or know that they have a dual diagnosis of another mental or physical illness, seek sound information and support so you can be armed with ways to further care for them. Most importantly, do not give up hope or become discouraged when faced with the complication and difficulty of having to support someone with a dual diagnosis. These survival stories show us that recovery from an eating disorder – and sometimes more than one – and an accompanying diagnosis is entirely possible.

Shame

Shame is the word used by a number of the survivors to describe how they felt about having an eating disorder. This saw many of them keep their intensely negative thoughts and internal voice, as well as their behaviours such as purging, not eating or overexercising to themselves. This created further concerns about denial and wanting to accept help, as it meant needing to face the reality of what was really going on: they had an eating disorder that required professional support.

'An aura of silence and avoidance surrounded me, which only served to increase my feelings of shame and isolation.' Kylie Rose

'I still didn't even think I was sick!' Ally

Recovery Reflections

While there have been many inroads made into reducing the stigma associated with mental illness, there is still much to be done in how it is perceived and therefore experienced by those suffering. Experiencing a mental illness such as an eating disorder or acute anxiety does not illicit the same level of compassion or understanding from some in the community as does an illness like cancer or even a painful and incapacitating broken limb.

There is no shame in experiencing an illness that no one could ever deliberately bring upon themselves and is so often a result of factors entirely outside the sufferer's control, such as genetics, cognitive disposition and a history of family mental illness. Carers can play a key role in encouraging the person they love to not just feel but know that the illness they are experiencing is nothing to be ashamed of, and that it can be treated.

Hospitalisation

Eating disorders are often dismissed as lightweight concerns of privileged young girls, which can be 'snapped out of'. Nothing could be further from the truth. This is a disorder that kills people and is undoubtedly life-threatening in many cases. Many of the survivors speak about their experiences of being hospitalised, and the trauma, loneliness and isolation they felt as a result should help dispel any myths that an eating disorder is not a serious illness or one that a person would willingly choose. Their experiences highlight how far we still have to go in getting inpatient care standards to a point where someone's emotional and psychological care is seen to be as important as their physical care and a return to physical health. A great deal more attention needs to be paid to inpatients' emotional healing while at the same time honouring the fact that it is absolutely vital for those in extreme circumstances to receive the nutritional restoration their body and mind require.

Despite improvements in inpatient care since some of these survivors were hospitalised, it should be noted that many describe traumatic stays where they received no counselling and limited visits by loved ones, even parents, as little as fifteen years ago.

'The month I was there was the most traumatic of my life.' Hannah

'I spent most of my day behind the nurses' desk being punished.' Emma Kate

Recovery Reflection

If your loved one requires a hospital admission to help them in their recovery from an eating disorder, they will require your intensive support, care and love to help them through that time, just as with any illness that requires hospitalisation. Hospitalisations for eating disorders, as these stories show, can be very lengthy and many people are often on total bed rest, being fed with a sometimes painful nasogastric tube. It can be a frightening and constricting experience, but at the same time one that is necessary to assist with nutritional restoration or even save their life.

Offer all the comfort and reassurance you possibly can. Do not be afraid to tell medical staff that you want to be made aware of everything that is happening in relation to your loved one's treatment, progress and post-discharge care. If old enough to participate in decisions, involve your loved one in all of these processes so they can be as empowered as possible about their own health and recovery and feel like they are part of the team that is helping to build them up and tear their eating disorder down.

Suicidal Tendencies

It is an unfortunate reality that some people experiencing an eating disorder self-harm and deal with suicidal thoughts on a regular basis. It is an even greater tragedy that sometimes these behaviours and thoughts translate into actual suicide attempts and suicides.

This makes eating disorders highly dangerous and turbulent mental illnesses that require close monitoring, support and professional help. Sometimes signs can be subtle and too easily missed, so even a hint of suicidal thoughts from a loved one should be taken seriously. The eating disorder voice and mindset can be manipulative, destructive and incredibly powerful in sending messages that someone is unlovable and unworthy to the point where they believe they do not deserve to live. When this is combined with other torturous thoughts and feelings, the pull towards self-harm and suicide can be frighteningly strong.

'By the time I was fourteen, my mood was much worse and I attempted suicide.' Nikki

'I became suicidal and desperately wanted to end my life to escape the pain I was feeling.' Kylie Rose

Recovery Reflection

Do not ever be afraid to ask a loved one if they are having suicidal thoughts, have a plan to suicide or have attempted suicide. Talking openly about this will not give them the idea or drive them to hurt themselves. Rather, it will show them that you are not afraid to talk about the deepest and darkest part of the torture they are experiencing and that you are fully there for them. Many people who do feel suicidal or are having suicidal thoughts want someone to fully realise the extent of what is happening to them but are afraid to open up for fear of the response. Create the most open and loving line of communication you can and, even though you may be frightened if they do say they are having these thoughts, remain calm and let them know you are there and will immediately begin the process of getting specialised help. Once this help is in place for your loved one, do not hesitate to seek assistance for yourself, or indeed at any other point in time while taking on the often difficult and emotionally draining role of being a carer.

If it is ever apparent that your loved one is in immediate danger from themselves, call for professional assistance urgently. Ring their doctor or counsellor, but if they are unavailable at the time, do not hesitate in calling 000 emergency services for help and advice.

Recovery Tips

If you're reading this book and you have an eating disorder, I hope that the recovery stories and tips it contains can help guide you towards taking small, or even large, steps to regaining your life and being eating disorder free. These tips have been written especially for you from the strong hearts and wise experiences of people who have been where you are right now – wondering what to do and how you might be able to begin a path to be free from an eating disorder.

Each has shared tips they used in becoming well, tips that you can now take and use in your own journey, knowing they are tried and true. While many of the tips are unique to each survivor, I don't believe it's a coincidence that many have written similar thoughts on the most powerful things to do and ways to recover.

The following are the main themes that came out of their messages of hope and recovery. They are yours to use to give you strategy, strength, power and self-love in overcoming your eating disorder and returning to your true self.

Do Things You Love

'Doing things you love is at the heart of your true purpose.' Anna

Engaging in loved activities, whatever they may be, is a key component to recovery and leading a full and happy life. An eating disorder will attempt to take away your desire to want to do fun and uplifting things, or even tell you that you are not worthy of having such joy in your life. This is not true and shutting yourself off from doing things you love will only make you sicker. Immerse yourself in loved activities as much as you possibly can, and push back against any notion that you don't deserve to do fun and positive things. You absolutely do.

Creativity

'Harnessing your creative powers can be incredibly powerful and vital.' Sophie

Many people who have experienced an eating disorder appear to have a very strong connection to creative forces and expression. Having a creative outlet such as music, drawing, singing, acting, blogging, writing or designing can not only be fun and enjoyable, it can play a direct role in your healing. Expressing yourself through writing, singing or art can articulate feelings you may be struggling to verbalise, thereby giving yourself another outlet for positive expression.

Embracing Imperfection

'Life goes on if something is not exact.' Emma Kate

Letting go of the need to be perfect both in behaviour and as a person may be a very important step in your recovery. A deep longing for perfection is a powerful force in the development of many eating disorders, always culminating in disappointment and self-rejection because there is no such thing as a perfect person, body, character or life. Embracing and trying to move towards happiness and self-fulfilment is a much more realistic and attainable life goal that will see you looking for ways to not only find joy in your life but lead you to understand that our flaws and imperfections are what make us human, relatable and lovable.

Intuitive, Gentle Eating

'Learning to accept myself and eat in a way that is intuitive and mindful was a profound help.' Laura

Recovery from an eating disorder can be much more than just the restoration of a nutritious diet and the absence of torturous feelings about food. Developing a relationship with food that is mindful, intuitive and even loving, is absolutely possible. If you have not heard about the benefits of mindful or intuitive eating it is worth exploring for the peaceful relationship with food it promotes. There is potential for this kind of eating to not only support you in your eating disorder recovery but also allow you to have a confident relationship with food for the rest of your life.

No Dieting

'Don't diet, no matter what your weight.' Michelle

Don't diet, or stop dieting. So many times the rapid descent people experience when in the early stages of an eating disorder can be traced back to the starting of a diet, particularly at a time of low self-esteem. We are surrounded by a dieting culture with little information and education given about how dangerous all restrictive diets are, not just those that are outrageously faddish. There really is no such thing as a safe diet that has weight loss as its purpose, particularly for any person suffering from low self-esteem and negative body image.

If you are overly concerned about your weight, appearance or body, the answer is not a diet. The answer is to find out why you feel this way in the first place – often the answer comes with much self-learning, growth and confidence building, through developing a relationship with a caring counselling professional.

No Comparisons

'Don't compare the way you look to models or indeed anyone.' Kirsty

Don't compare your personality, your body or your life to anyone else's. You are a unique and worthy person just because you exist. No matter what an eating disorder or anyone else may tell you, you have the right to just 'be' and not feel compelled to compare your life, achievements or body to others'. Such comparisons never bode favourably for anyone experiencing low self-esteem or an eating disorder, and serve only as a vehicle to put yourself or others down.

You do not need to be, act or look like anyone else. Even if you feel disheartened, sick or even broken, you just need to be you. Accepting yourself for who you are and where you are right now will allow you to take that self-love in and move forwards with your life; regardless of whether you still wish to make changes to be a happier and more confident person.

Don't Be Ashamed

'It is not a shameful or embarrassing thing to have an eating disorder.' Elizabeth

There is nothing to be ashamed about if you are experiencing an eating disorder or indeed any other mental illness. Such thinking only keeps you unwell and possibly feeds into thinking you are not as unwell as you really are or that you don't need to seek professional help.

In their lifetime, every person experiences issues they need assistance with, and many times that means seeking out and utilising professional help. People who reach out for help are not weak. They are, in fact, showing great strength and emotional intelligence in directly addressing an issue that is stopping them from living their life to its fullest.

Back Yourself

'I was the one who had to make the decision to support and back myself.' Mitchell

While professional help and the love of family and friends can play a key role in helping you recover from your eating disorder, to be fully well again you must 'turn up' for yourself and back yourself to get well. You have to be on your own side and cannot expect everyone else to believe in you if you don't believe in yourself.

While this can be difficult if pushing against a negative inner voice and depressive mindset, turning up for yourself is an action and belief that can be seen in sometimes the smallest of things, such as keeping therapy appointments, talking to friends or doing a loved activity.

Let Love In

'Reach out and seek help.' Michelle

Don't push others away who are trying to help you; let the love they have for you in. Accept help when offered and allow others to support you. You are not alone and do not have to go through your recovery alone either. There are people surrounding you who want to help, and even if you think that's not true given your own family and friendship circumstances, there are other ways to reach out for professional help or support and guidance in pro-recovery communities. Seek them out on social networks like Twitter and

Facebook or at targeted pro-recovery and mentoring websites. These communities can provide you with inspiration, positive thought, guidance and, yes, even love when you need it most.

Love is everywhere and you are permitted to have your share.

Separation

'Find ways to separate the real you from the illness because it is absolutely not who you are.' Elise

You are not your eating disorder. You were not born to suffer or endure its misery. You were born to think and be and do what *you* want, not what an eating disorder wants. This is why learning to separate yourself from the eating disorder, and especially the negative inner voice it might be criticising you with, is so important.

When you hear or even feel within yourself those times when the 'real' you is talking – either out loud or inside your head – take special note of what you are doing, who you are with and how you are feeling. Find ways to both nurture and replicate that 'real-ness', because it is that *real you* who will make positive decisions and take small steps towards your recovery. If you are struggling to hear that real and encouraging voice because the eating disorder is so loud, be gently guided by a professional and your loved ones, and by what is the true and beautiful you, rather than the thoughts and actions of the eating disorder. The more you find, nurture, believe and follow your real voice, the more the eating disorder voice will quieten and fade away.

One Step at a Time

'All journeys require you to take one step and one day at a time. Don't place too much pressure on yourself to try and race ahead with your recovery.'
Jessica

Don't place pressure on yourself to heal from your eating disorder overnight or even too quickly. We can all only take one step at a time in anything we do in life and sometimes those steps may be quite small. This is absolutely OK. Keep moving forwards no matter how slow your recovery may seem.

Also be mindful to not compare your journey with anyone else's. We can all draw strength and hope from others who may have been in a similar situation but your path in recovery, as in life, is truly your own. Do not judge yourself on the size of the steps you are taking towards recovery. Actually taking those steps is at the heart of what matters to your health and wellbeing, not the size of them.

Self-love

'Learning to love and accept yourself is a key part of eating disorder recovery.' Faye

Learning to love and believe in yourself will shut your eating disorder out. The negativity of an eating disorder cannot thrive in someone who believes they are worthy and valuable. Such thinking will sometimes slowly, but sometimes quickly, drown an eating disorder out or starve it of the belief it needs to keep its grip on you.

Learning to build your self-esteem and treat yourself with loving compassion will help your heart heal. It will also see you love and honour your body in such a way that you will feel compelled to treat it well. A powerful thing to work towards and achieve not only for eating disorder recovery, but for a life well loved and lived.

Non-Linear Recovery

'Be forgiving of yourself, especially as your recovery path may see you take steps backwards and sideways, as well as forwards.' Solveig

Very few things, if any, follow a straight path in life and this is also true for recovery journeys from an eating disorder. Understand and be OK with the fact that your recovery is not linear and you will likely take many steps forwards, backwards and sideways. You may even at times feel like you have relapsed entirely, but if you have already had the experience of what it is like to move forwards, then you will never truly go back to where you once were.

Be OK with the bumps and turns that recovery may bring and never think that you aren't 'doing it right' or that you're 'getting it wrong'. Now is not the time, nor is it ever, to beat yourself up. It's OK and normal for there to be small and even large setbacks on a recovery path. It does not mean you can't recover or have to start all over again.

Surround Yourself with Inspiration

'You deserve to be surrounded by beauty, colour and inspiration.' Emma Kate

You are on an inspirational path to recovery and wellness, and on such a journey you deserve to be surrounded with beautiful things that further boost this inspiration. Read inspirational books, seek out and use positive affirmations, surround yourself with favourite quotes and beautiful things and read uplifting content online. This will be a shield against the negativity of an eating disorder and build you up as a positive recovery warrior at the same time.

Professional Help

'There is someone out there for you who can help and if you haven't found them, keep searching.' Hannah

Seek professional help. No one is ever expected to battle a serious illness such as an eating disorder by themselves. Seeking help as early as possible, before you feel completely out of control or taken over by an eating disorder, is a vital step in recovery. Counselling therapies are particularly important, but so are others that are alternative in nature or have a focus on nutritional restoration and assistance. While early assistance is vital, this does not mean that professional help will not work for you if you have been suffering with an eating disorder for a long time. Nothing could be further from the truth. If you are willing to support yourself by reaching out for help and beginning a path to recovery, you too can be well. It is never too late.

While in some instances a positive and trusting connection to just one professional person who knows how to treat eating disorders can be key to recovery, so can a team of professionals all working together with you at its heart. Such a team, combined with your belief and will, is a powerful force in tearing an eating disorder down and ridding it from your life.

Don't Minimise

'If you know in your heart that you are experiencing difficulties with food, don't get too caught up in a diagnosis and especially not the thinking that you may not be as sick as someone else.' George

Don't ever think of yourself as not sick enough to get help. You do not need to be very thin or emaciated to seek help for your eating disorder, nor do you have to be at the point where you are filled with torturous thoughts about yourself, your body or food. If people you know and trust are saying they are worried about you, or you are beginning to realise that something is not right, then it's not. Even if there is only a faint whisper of a voice heard every now and again that tells you something is not right and that you should tell someone or get help, you *must listen.* This is your voice, not the eating disorder's voice, and it deserves to be respected and heard.

Kindness

'Be patient, gentle and kind with yourself.' Kylie
Rose

Treating yourself with loving kindness is an absolutely
necessary component to you getting well. Your eating
disorder is being harsh and cruel to you, and you will
need to be gentle and nurturing to yourself in every possible way to squash its power. You must show yourself
the compassion the eating disorder believes you are not
worthy of. By doing so you will starve it of the self-hate
it needs to live. You'll kill it with love.

Whatever helps to promote this kindness within
you is important for you to do. It may be as simple
as sleeping, a gentle walk, stopping putting yourself down, or spending time with trusted and loved
people. Let others also be kind to you, especially
if you're struggling to do so yourself. Allow others
to show how much they care for you and let them
be a part of your recovery team.

Worthiness

'Don't for one moment believe that recovery is
something that is meant to be for everyone else except yourself.' George

You are worthy of recovery. Every person is. Don't ever
believe, despite what an eating disorder voice may be
telling you, that you must live with an eating disorder.
This is your life and you, as much as anyone else, deserve to live it free and in the way you choose to.

Do not let the eating disorder or anyone else take away or minimise the belief that you are worthy of recovery. Any thought, person, experience or feeling that prompts that within you is a warning sign to be dealt with so that the real you holds on to the belief you are always worthy of working towards an eating disorder-free life.

Hope

'Anything, including recovery, is possible when you have hope.' Jessica

Have hope.
Hold on.
Believe.
With hope that you can be well – anything is possible.
And it is.

Transcending

Faye's Story

Born to be a performer, highly successful TV presenter and fashion designer, Faye, has lived much of her life in the spotlight. A teenage experience of anorexia, while seemingly dealt with at the time, was to come back to Faye at the height of her career and while she was in a volatile relationship. A chance meeting and now daily meditation contributed significantly to her healing, allowing her to continue her high-profile career.

I'm a seventies love child, born in London to a British mumma and rock and roll Aussie dad. My parents were madly in love when they had me, and moved to Brisbane in Queensland when I was one. Growing up, I was a classic daddy's girl but I got along with and loved Mum too. We were a great trio.

I was a bright little girl but always felt afraid to show my intelligence because I was scared of being different and standing out. In one of my earliest school classes I was asked to count from one to a hundred, which I knew how to do, but I made a mistake on purpose at ninety-eight because I was afraid I would be judged if I got it right. I did like school and had nice friends, but that nagging insecurity always seemed to be with me. Despite, or maybe because of it, I was gregarious and quite a performer.

I was good at drama and singing, but that too was a concern for me as I felt if I was too good at it, other kids would not like me. I was afraid no one would want to be my friend and that they would be jealous if I excelled. This jealousy did actually happen in my final year of school, when I got my first job in television. It was almost like a self-fulfilling prophecy – something I knew was going to happen.

Puberty was a difficult time for me chiefly because I became aware my parents' relationship was ending. There was late-night shouting, crying and fighting. It was an awful time and the sense of security I previously felt I had around me vanished. I felt out of control and no longer knew where my safety net was. They officially separated when I was eleven and Mumma was the one to leave home. Dad and Grandma told me she was the problem in the relationship and I believed them. As a result I didn't talk to her for a number of years. I did see her sometimes, but mostly my life was just with Dad. I pushed Mumma away only because I was confused and looking for someone to blame. I missed her every day.

I went to an Anglican all-girl high school, which was challenging. It was very regimented and there was no sense of fun with learning. It was highly competitive and I felt all my creative passions, which had been nurtured at primary school, were stripped away. I lost my connection to the creative part of myself and I felt like a little ant in a big colony. The first year was

OK but after that I felt the girls around me became incredibly competitive about their bodies and academically, which made me feel self-conscious.

Growing up, I was a little fish and loved to swim. I had to be pulled out of the water or told not to go in if it was freezing cold, but in high school, swimming became my most hated subject. When standing on the blocks to dive in, girls would look at your body, specifically your legs, to see if you had a gap between them. If you did you were acceptable. If you didn't, you weren't. I suddenly found myself making up excuses not to swim and be seen in my bathers as I didn't have that gap.

There was a culture at the school that being thin equalled success and popularity. Fat was bad and seen as unacceptable and not cool. I started to exercise and eat healthily in response to what I saw and felt happening around me. I didn't do anything too strenuous to begin with, but one day I overheard a girl at school say, 'Faye's lost a lot of weight. She looks really good, doesn't she?' Another girl then said, 'Yeah. But I reckon she could lose even more.' At that moment, something snapped inside my head. My thinking about my body and what I was eating changed dramatically. I was thirteen and in my first year of high school.

I instantly developed a drive to lose weight and believed I wasn't good enough until I did so. Thinking about it now, I recognise how ridiculous that thinking was and that I should have just said, 'Screw you!' to all of them and that I was fine and happy as I was. But I was in a vulnerable phase of my life with my parents separating and I reached out for a sense of control in an effort to get some validation. When I did start to lose weight it got me more attention at school. Girls would ask what I was doing to lose weight, which they thought was great. A friend and I even decided to diet together; I now know that was a horrible thing for us to do, but we thought we were helping one another.

The change in my thinking was strong, urgent and instant. I became obsessed with wanting to be thin. I felt like I had no control over my life with my family breaking up, going through puberty and what was happening at school. I began to barely eat and would exercise furiously whenever I could. Dad didn't notice the change in me straight away, despite the fact I lost a lot of weight very quickly.

My physical education teacher was the first person to notice there was an issue. She asked me if I was eating but it was the wrong question to ask. I wish she'd asked, 'Are you OK, Faye?' or, 'How are you?', so that I could open up and tell someone what I was feeling. Instead I became defensive and refused to talk about what I was eating. It fuelled me to want to be even thinner and by now my thinking was incredibly destructive. The drive to be thin and lose more weight took over my every thought.

I started to swim more because I now had the coveted gap between my legs. It became something I wanted to show off to prove to the other girls that I was disciplined and acceptable. I didn't have a strongly negative voice inside my head at the time, but I do remember a strong whisper of praise when my body became thinner. For me, it was always more of a feeling that I was fat and unacceptable and that I had to do something to fix myself. I was often incredibly hungry and after starving for a week or more I would not be able to take it so I would binge and then purge.

I got a boyfriend in my mid teens and he slowly noticed my weight loss. He didn't know how to handle it and would joke to my friends about me needing to eat, so I would pretend to eat around him. My best friend then started to notice I wasn't eating, but I did everything to avoid the questioning. By the time I was fifteen, my parents realised something wasn't right and Dad became incredibly angry with me and started to be bossy about what I was eating. I wanted him to ask me what was wrong, but he kept asking me what I was eating. We battled each other for a while but I then got to such a low weight that he took me to a doctor.

This was around the time of my school formal and I was having a dress made. The first time I tried it on I thought I looked good, but every fitting after that the dress got bigger and bigger on me. Dad dragged to me to the doctor while I insisted nothing was wrong. When the doctor weighed me and told me I would be put in hospital if I didn't start to eat, I got frightened and immediately checked back in with more rational thoughts. I didn't know what an eating disorder was. I believed I could keep doing what I was doing and be fine, but clearly I couldn't. I also thought what was happening to me was just the pressure I felt from the other girls and it was no big deal. I was told I was very sick and that it was a matter of life and death if I didn't start to eat.

I'd wanted attention but not this kind. I couldn't understand why everyone was being so aggressive towards me. Dad was angry. The doctor was angry. Everyone around me seemed to be angry with me. Dad yelled at me a lot and told me I was ridiculous and just needed to eat. It wasn't what I wanted to hear but I wanted to please him and felt I had to fix it and make things right.

At my final dress fitting before the formal I remember looking at myself in the mirror and thinking: 'That's enough. You're too skinny.' I actually saw myself properly for the first time as others around me were seeing me. Even though I hated Dad yelling at me, in many ways I think it helped me to get a reality check and understand that I needed to stop punishing my body and myself.

At this time, Mumma had a baby girl and she was the catalyst for us beginning to talk again. Sarah was a little angel who brought us back together and I wanted to visit Mumma regularly because of the baby, who I adored. I also found out at this time about an opportunity to do some work experience in TV, something I had always wanted to do. It really excited me and helped to shift my thoughts to be kinder and more focused on my health, rather than being thin. I began to eat and take better care of myself as I now felt I had an amazing goal to reach for.

I slowly started to eat and think more positively and I did work experience at Channel Ten in the news-room and on a children's television show called *Totally Wild*, which was about the environment and animals. I did a small story for them and from that was offered a job on the show. They saw talent in me and it was an environment where my creativity was encour-aged. This hadn't been happening at school and so I felt like I had landed myself in an amazing place.

I was offered a presenting role for *Totally Wild* and as soon as I finished my final year of school, I started. I even did a few stories for them while I was in my second last year of school. I was eating disorder free during this time and felt good about my body. I occasionally had to be mindful of not exercising too much but I had a focus and something that gave me direction and this helped me no end.

Even though it was incredible to be offered a TV presenting job while so young, it caused me enormous grief at school. Other girls became extremely jealous and were verbally abusive and wrote the most horrible things about me on the back of bathroom doors. I told Dad and he offered to talk to the school but I didn't want him to as I thought it would cause trouble. He helped me to realise I had succeeded on my own and that it was an achievement and to forget them. His words really helped me to think about what I had achieved and I decided to instead throw myself into this amazing job I had at just seventeen.

I started presenting on *Totally Wild* full time and I loved that I was both creatively responsible and encouraged in my work. It gave me so many skills and an amazing toolkit of knowledge, not to mention I got to travel around Australia. I presented for *Totally Wild* for nearly ten years and in that time I coped really well with being on TV from a body image perspective. I took incredibly good care of myself as I knew I had to be well to keep the job. I loved it so much I didn't want anything to stand in the way of that happening. I would have days every now and again where I didn't feel as confident about myself as I would have liked, but overall I felt good about myself. I also had a long-term boyfriend during this time and, even though we eventually broke up, it was a positive relationship for me.

When I made the decision to leave *Totally Wild*, some of the eating disorder thinking and behaviours came back to me and I was soon to realise the show had been a wonderful ten-year distraction but that I had never really dealt with why I'd become sick in the first place. I was sad to leave the show but, now in my mid twenties, I felt like I was ready for the next challenge in my life. I went to London for a holiday and when I returned, the producers asked me to do six months again on the show, but this time from Sydney. I had always wanted to live in Sydney and so did the stint. At the end I wanted to stay but the show wanted me to return to Brisbane. It was time for us to move on without one another.

When I moved to Sydney I started to become more interested in the TV social scene, which I had never been previously. Sydney was more of a party town, but despite going to lots of parties and media events I never felt the need to court media attention. It was just a time for me to have fun and meet new people in a city where I knew barely anyone. Despite having fun going out, I was soon to realise that finding work was not easy.

Everyone knew me as the *Totally Wild* girl and despite doing a lot of auditions, I found myself very typecast. After six months, I eventually found work on three different shows, all of them related to home, lifestyle and renovation. It was great to be presenting again but I knew in my heart I wasn't really fulfilled and something was missing in my life. I didn't have a great deal of creativity in what I was doing, which was the part of my heart that really needed to speak. As a result, some of my eating disorder behaviours returned and were heightened by the volatile relationship I was now in.

Looking back, I realise that my first relationship after I moved to Sydney came to teach me a life lesson, although at the time I wished I was anywhere but experiencing the pain it brought to my life. I don't believe it is a coincidence I found myself with a man who was very obsessed with his appearance, body and image. It did not take long before his insecurities fed mine.

I became obsessed with being as lean as I could be, afraid that if I wasn't, he would leave me. Our relationship was negative and while I thought I loved him for the six years we were together, I think it was more a magnetic obsession of our two minds, or a physical attraction and not a loving relationship at all. We became engaged but deep in my heart I knew it wasn't right and we eventually broke up over something silly.

I had started to see a holistic counsellor while still engaged because I was so unhappy. I discussed my negative body image as well as my relationship, but I found talking about things incredibly confronting. We tried cognitive behavioural therapy and neuro-linguistic programming but I didn't feel like it was helping, so I went to see a kinesiologist. Some days I thought it was helping me, but again I couldn't really feel the benefit. I then tried another kinesiologist who was also a counsellor, and I came to understand I was accepting less than I should in my relationship. Even though I don't think I was aware of it at the time, I am sure that helped me to leave the relationship.

I now felt completely lost. I had lost so much of myself and there were days to come where I felt so alone and wretched I wanted to rip off my skin. I no longer knew who I was or where I wanted to go, be, or even do. It was a swirl of dark confusion. One day I was walking home crying when a woman passed by me and asked if I was OK. Incredibly, she lived in my street and we talked. I miraculously felt like I could trust her and as we talked she suggested I try transcendental meditation to help me be more at peace with my thoughts. Thinking I had nothing to lose, I decided to try it, never knowing it was to change my life.

As I learned to meditate and understand the benefits of focusing my thoughts, I learned to be accepting of the ebbs and flows in my life and open my mind to more love and possibilities. It helped me process the pain of my relationship and healed the negative thoughts I had about my body. It has also taught me what my body needs and what makes me feel good and what doesn't.

Prior to learning to meditate I was thinking about myself in such negative ways and treating myself badly as well. Transcendental meditation has taught me to love myself and never accept less than what I am worth in any aspect of my life. I see a healer on occasion now and the thing I love most about our work together is that we don't dwell in the past, but focus on my thoughts and feelings in the present. We are focused on how I feel and behave now and what I need to do to make things better. My healer has studied all over the world and I enjoy and benefit from our time together immeasurably.

After my relationship ended, I became determined to find and nurture my creative side again and I found myself drawn to fashion. Fashion had always been something I'd loved and I regularly read fashion magazines, escaping into their colour and language. I love the way fashion journalists write about fabrics, styles and inspirations. I was never very interested in models as some people are. For me it was always about the clothes. I see models for what they are. They have a job to do but I don't see them as any more beautiful than someone who is not a model.

I started a fashion label called Love Chile, which was my attempt to feel free and alive again. It began as a notion to heal myself and as I went down that path, it became clear to me that a lot of other women needed healing too. My first collection was a range of T-shirts with inspirational messages, and at this time I began to do some ambassadorial work with the Butterfly Foundation.

I wanted to reach out to others who were experiencing negative body image or eating disorders and as I did so I became amazed that there were so many people who didn't love and accept themselves. I wanted to help and do something to change that, and speaking at a Butterfly event recently was a revelation to me. As I was speaking about my years of low self-worth and loathing I noticed there were so many women nodding and even crying at my story and, afterwards, telling me they had similar feelings. It was an amazing experience and I want to do it more.

As well as Love Chile, I taught at the National Institute of Dramatic Art, which I loved, presented infomercials and was the face of a car insurance company. You may have seen me pop up on TV most mornings on Kerri-Anne Kennerley, *The Circle*, *The Morning Show* and in ads on Foxtel. Love Chile has been very successful and has appeared in many fashion magazines and I have now created *Fashion Hound*, interviewing other designers, fashion muses and even people on the street about the role fashion plays in their life. For me it is the perfect balance of storytelling and presenting. Being a fashion journalist and designer is a dream come true for me. I wanted to make it happen and I am proud I created it for myself using social media as the sole form of connection with readers and commenters. I write, produce, shoot, edit and present *Fashion Hound* and I love it.

The most helpful thing in my recovery was undoubtedly transcendental meditation. I feel so connected to it that I know I will practice it for the rest of my life. The only time I miss it is if I am really sick and need to sleep or totally rest. It always makes me feel so centred, and I want to keep learning and getting better at it. I had a wonderful teacher, which really helped, and he has taught me that just twenty minutes of quiet meditation and reflection morning and night can bring untold richness to my life.

It is so important for anyone suffering from an eating disorder to know that they are worthy of help. We all need help with aspects of our lives sometimes and being ravaged by low self-esteem and damaging thoughts is certainly one of those times. I truly believe my eating disorder has taught me it is a sign of strength to reach out for help and talk to someone. And that life is for living and not for being introspective and hating yourself. In many ways, I have to thank it for that as I can't be sure I would have learned to love and honour myself as I do now if it was not for the experience. That's certainly something to be grateful for.

Faye's Recovery Tips

1. Don't be silent. It is OK to tell people what you are thinking and feeling, even if those thoughts and emotions are frightening. People love you and want to help and you should let them in.
2. Learning to love and accept yourself is a key part of eating disorder recovery. I'm not sure it is fully possible without self-acceptance, so finding ways to explore how you can love yourself is incredibly important.
3. Don't be hard on yourself if you take a step backwards or even fully relapse. Life constantly throws us curve balls and every time you are tested, you are bound to learn more about yourself and what triggers and upsets you. Each experience can make you stronger if you choose to see it that way rather than be defeated.
4. If you are filled with negative thoughts or find it difficult to control your thinking, consider learning a form of meditation. It can help you focus on your heart and soul, which will drown out the negativity you may be experiencing. It takes practice and commitment but it's worth it.
5. Every time you get dressed you become a living, breathing work of art. Wear colours that make you feel bright and happy, shoes that put a spring in

your step, jewellery that makes you feel fabulous and clothes that honour your true self. Fashion can be fun and liberating and is a great way for you to express yourself to tell your story through style.

Acknowledgement

Kylie Rose's Story

Kylie Rose's journey highlights how bullying can have a devastating and lasting impact on a young person's life – to the point where it drives them to mental illness. After suffering years of systematic schoolyard bullying, Kylie Rose developed a life-threatening eating disorder. With the help of not only an outstanding counsellor, but a legal team, she courageously faced her illness head on and beat it.

I know a lot of people dream about making a sea change. They want a quieter, more relaxing life, free of city stress and pressure. When my parents and I moved from inner city Melbourne to a farm in eastern Victoria when I was ten, this was exactly what we hoped for and got – but not for long. After the first two years of a carefree resettlement we began to experience more stress, worry and pain than we ever had before, none of which were in our sea change plans.

I had enjoyed school and my life in Melbourne prior to our move. I was a happy child, always in the middle of everything, with lots of friends. As an only child, I was very good at occupying myself and I was a prolific daydreamer and reader who loved to create artistic things. When my parents told me that we were moving to the country to live on a cattle farm and be nearer to my grandparents and other family, I was genuinely excited.

I loved the farm, which was only a ten-minute walk from my new primary school. Town was a fifteen-minute drive away. On weekends, I would ride my bike, make little documentaries with my video camera, catch frogs and run around. It was an idyllic lifestyle and I loved my new school. It was a tiny primary school with only thirty students and we got a lot of personal attention and encouragement. I made nice friends and managed to sail through the early stages of puberty well. I was very childlike and not overly aware of my growing body in any major way. It wasn't even a factor for me and I don't think it was for my friends either. I had an open relationship with both my mum and dad and I loved them dearly.

This all changed dramatically before the end of the following year, my first in high school. The first semester was exciting and fun, but after going out with a boy for a day in one of those silly schoolyard romances, things went horribly wrong. He publicly dumped me before the end of the day and started teasing me about my appearance. I should have known it was coming, as within hours of going out with him I immediately found there was pressure on me sexually, not just from him, but from everyone around me. It seemed to be seen as a rite of passage and I had no idea how to react. I was inexperienced and shy and knew it didn't feel right. From this day on, the boy continued to tease me seemingly in an attempt to impress his mates. It wasn't long before they joined in.

The bullying continued for the remainder of that year and throughout the next. After such a prolonged period of teasing, my previously positive self-esteem was destroyed. Because they were so fixated on my appearance, I became that way too. I started to diet and I constantly worried about what I looked like. I would look in a mirror and see exactly the horrible things they were calling me. Many times they would tease me and then come-on to me, which made me feel conflicted and afraid. I felt powerless in deflecting their ridicule and it undermined my ability to feel safe at school and within my own skin.

I started to look at teen magazines and compare myself to models. I thought if I looked like them the bullies would stop targeting me. I began to eat less and intrusive thoughts about food and how to avoid eating began to take over my thinking. At the time it helped me to block out what was happening to me, which was too over-whelming to deal with. On the surface I wanted to lose weight to look like the models I had become focused on, but beneath this I was trying to control my body and fade away.

I felt incredibly helpless and dreaded attending school. I stopped going out with friends and began to exercise frenetically. By now I was also hearing a loud and punishing voice inside in my head, which relent-lessly shouted that I was ugly and not good enough. It constantly criticised me and amplified everything the boys were telling me a hundred times over. I had the outside telling me exactly what the inside was telling me and vice versa. It was a powerful combination that slowly tore me down.

I was incredibly ashamed of what had been taking place and felt like I couldn't tell my parents. I didn't even know how to describe it and felt I must have done something to deserve it too. My pursuit for thinness was taking on a life of its own and I now found that my aversion to food was no longer within my realm of control but rather at the command of the voice. By the time Mum and Dad realised that something was not right, I had been unwell for nearly two years. I was now hopelessly sick both physically and mentally and they were shocked and had no idea what to say or do. My previously joyful disposition had disappeared, replaced by intense sadness and dramatic weight loss. I was a shell of my former self.

I was diagnosed with anorexia by a local doctor. It was a relief initially for us to better understand the chaos in which we had been living, but I quickly realised the eating disorder wasn't going to allow me to eat. Thinness had come to represent both a deterrent and a protective shield for me and I feared putting on weight and my body developing, which I felt would make the boys pay me more attention. Mum and Dad were devastated with my diagnosis but both immediately went into action. They took the exercise bike out of my room, encouraged me to pick up hobbies I used to enjoy and started to take control of what I was eating. I fought them constantly and the eating disorder was not a fan of anything they did. They were trying to pull me out of it and it was trying to keep me in its web.

My classmates knew I was sick but in general I was tiptoed around and ignored. No one asked me what was wrong and, because of the school's bullying culture and the stigma attached to eating disorders at the time, I was practically invisible. An aura of silence and avoidance surrounded me, which only served to increase my feelings of shame and isolation. The teasing continued but by now it was more about me being ill. They had teased me to the point where I became sick and then excluded me further for becoming so.

I went to see a local counsellor and continued to see the doctor. I did put on weight, but as soon as that happened I became bulimic. Once I began to eat again and got a taste for food, I began to binge and purge. The first time I purged I felt relieved. I had found something else I could do in secret that subdued my inner turmoil and self-loathing, but little did I know how lonely and painful bulimia can be. Midway through year nine I was sicker than ever and nothing was helping.

Mum rang a state-wide eating disorder service and they referred me to a Melbourne hospital to do an out-patient program. I lived with my aunty and cousins throughout the treatment and schoolwork was sent to me. I was there for a number of months and saw a team of professionals who did help me. I know, though, that the thing that saw me get well during that time was simply not being at school. I felt free for the first time in years. The fear the bullies were instilling in me was no longer there and everything in my life became easier. My parents visited often and I loved being around my cousins. The horrible voice inside my head slowly quietened.

While I was in Melbourne my mum found out from my closest friend that the boys were teasing me. She went to the school to demand an apology from the boy who was chiefly responsible. The school counsellor became involved and told him he had to say sorry, but he refused to say it in person, instead writing me a note. I was given the note and told by the counsellor that I was not to show it to anyone or talk about it or I would be accused of harassment too. This made me feel like I deserved what he had done to me and that he had gotten away with everything. Mum and I talked about what had been happening and while this did help a bit, I desperately wanted her to stop intervening as it was making the bullying worse.

After the summer I returned home ready for year ten, but on the first day a boy who was a part of the bullying group began sexually harassing me and I relapsed. Everything I had worked for in recovery fell apart. I lasted three weeks before starting to run away from school and having severe panic attacks. I began purging again. I became anxious about leaving the house and would get up at 3am to prepare myself for school, but still struggled to get there.

Eventually I could no longer get myself to school and had to stay at home with the escalating voice of the eating disorder inside my head. It was so disheartening to have come so far only to return to the same hostile environment and lose myself again. I became suicidal and desperately wanted to end my life to escape the pain I was feeling. The eating disorder had me in a trance-like state and I struggled to find any hope of being free from its tightening grip.

My parents didn't know what to do, because no matter what they said or did, the eating disorder had completely overpowered me. I'm sure they felt like they had lost their daughter as I was no longer responding to anyone and had completely shut down. By sixteen, I was a client of the regional psychiatric service and regularly being taken to hospital for suicide attempts and dehydration. All my friends were living their lives, going to movies and the beach, and I was living with an illness whose mission it seemed was to kill me. I felt like my life was slipping away and I was incredibly despondent that I couldn't share in normal teenage ventures with my friends.

My experiences in hospital were not always helpful. My mother overheard two nurses speaking about me one day, saying, 'Why is she in that bed? She's a waste of space. We could use that bed for someone who can't control what is happening to them and is really ill.' Mum was furious with them and the general perception was that I was a vain and spoilt brat who was seeking attention. My eating disorder was not seen as a life-threatening illness, rather as a lifestyle I had chosen and was in control of. If anyone had truly known the affliction I was experiencing, there is no way they would have thought that I – or indeed anyone – would choose the nightmare that is an eating disorder.

Miraculously, I managed to do some school work from home and in hospital, and by the start of year eleven I went back to school. I decided to write a letter to the boy apologising to him for him being made to apologise to me. I did it in the hope that it would appease him and make school a less threatening place to be. The bullying subsided somewhat and became not so much about verbal taunts, but exclusion.

It wasn't long before he and a few of his friends were excluding me from other students and, feeling trapped and unable to reach anyone, I found myself at the mercy of the eating disorder again. The school did nothing to support me despite knowing I was sick. The boys were still in control after all these years and no one questioned or held them accountable for their actions. In my immediate group of girlfriends, very few stood up for me and the rest, either through a desire to be affiliated with the boys or fear of being victimised themselves, joined in, or stood by and did nothing.

I continued to see psychiatric services but they had no idea what was going on at school, continually blaming my parents for the eating disorder. I felt like they never really listened, but rather told me what was at fault with me. I tried to tell them that my family life was a mess because of the eating disorder, not that family dysfunction had caused the eating disorder to emerge. I was petrified of attending school and yet no one thought that school might have been a problem. Instead, they stirred up guilt in my parents for being the reason I was sick. My eating disorder was not permitting me to speak easily and I needed someone gentle and caring to ask me the right questions.

By the end of the first term of year eleven we decided a change of school may help. I moved back to Melbourne with my grandmother to go to a girls' school but I was too sick to make it work. I stuck it out for a term but desperately wanted to go home. By this time I actually wanted to go back to school, but I was too afraid of what awaited me there. I worked at a fast food place in town for a while but soon gave that up when I found a peer of the boy worked there too.

I returned to Melbourne to live with another aunty and went to a university to finish my last year and a half of school. My aunty was wonderful and took great care of me, but I continued to struggle with the eating disorder even though I could now see I was very emaciated and ill. The best thing about this time was making a friend at university I felt comfortable enough with to talk to. When I told her about my experiences, she was supportive and told me what had been happening to me was not OK.

This empowered me to begin investigating the bullying further. I returned home and had now been suffering for six arduous years. Both my mind and body were very weak, but I was determined to find out more about what had been happening to me and why. My investigations led me to a law firm and I rang them to see if they could help me. They told me I could sue the school and that I had a great case. I decided to do it and my parents were supportive. For such a long time I felt like I didn't have a voice, but the law firm helped me find it. I needed to stand up for myself and take back my life. It was healing and freeing for me to write down everything that had taken place. I could finally give it to someone who was listening to me and who could do something with it too.

We sued the school in a five-year legal battle. I felt like I needed to do it to save my life and this really turned out to be the case. The trauma of the bullying and how it damaged my self-image was what was fuelling the eating disorder, and until I dealt with this, I knew I was never going to be fully well. As soon as I started to take control in this way I began to feel better. I stopped being a scared girl and became a young woman who refused to be a victim of cowardly bullies or an eating disorder anymore.

During the litigation I did a few small jobs and a traineeship in administration. The traineeship was positive and helped boost my confidence. I made friends at the job and felt more a part of the community where I lived. Slowly, I got well, especially after I found a great counsellor. She understood the mechanism of the eating disorder voice and helped me deal with the psychological effects of the bullying. It had taken me eight years, but I felt like I had found someone amazing who really listened to me. Her assistance was life changing and I looked forward to our sessions, where I wrote all her knowledge of eating disorders in a notebook. She also helped support me through the litigation, because while it was liberating on some levels, it was also very stressful.

Eventually, after five years and mediation, we settled out of court. The school said they were sorry and that they knew they had failed me. I felt that this was all I needed and that the vast weight I had been carrying for such a long time had finally been lifted off my shoulders. Just to have the acknowledgement that the years of bullying did in fact occur and they should have done something to intervene and help me; it felt like a missing piece of the puzzle had found its way to me. By then I felt I had endured all I could and just wanted to settle and move forwards with my life.

Now twenty-three, I found myself a woman by age

but certainly not by feeling or experience. There was a massive gap in my life and it was daunting to feel that reality. I had not had an adolescence and I felt very behind everyone else my age. A big piece of my life had been taken away from me and I had no idea how to embrace life when all I had known for such a long time was an eating disorder. I gave myself lots of time to slowly move through things and soon, life became the most beautiful and precious thing.

I surrounded myself with optimistic people and this helped me to attain a more positive view of myself. Over the years I had become apprehensive of trusting anyone, so dating was difficult, but that too became easier with time. Now instead of only viewing my eating disorder as a negative experience, I endeavoured to give it positive meaning. I was gentler with myself and with an open and hopeful heart I took recovery one step and one day at a time. With a newfound sense of wellness, I moved to Melbourne to live with a cousin and start studying psychology at university. I finally felt independent, in charge of my life and very much like myself again.

I can now eat whatever I feel like and am living a normal life like other young women my age. I feel more comfortable with myself and who I am and I have established my identity as Kylie Rose. Life has become a great deal more wonderful without the eating disorder's voice consuming my spirit. I'm meeting lots of new people and the world feels like it is opening up to me. I read for leisure and love to go shopping and I'm learning more about myself and uncovering new passions. I once wished for a life without an eating disorder when it seemed like an impossibility, but today that wish is a reality, and it's a beautiful place to be.

The most helpful thing in recovery for me was separating the eating disorder voice from my own and learning to distinguish its distortions and messages from reality. Coming to understand that I wasn't a horrible person, rather that I had a horrible illness, helped me enormously. I know the eating disorder well enough now to challenge it and rationalise against its voice. I know now my voice is stronger and that I am not ugly or bad like it tries to convince me. I know I do need to be mindful of being stressed and I manage that by listening to beautiful music, going for gentle walks and talking things through with friends.

Although more attention is being paid to it now, the devastating impact that bullying can have on a child or young person shouldn't be underestimated. I was driven into and kept in my eating disorder by systematic verbal, emotional, exclusionary and sexual bullying. I understand now that I was always susceptible to the illness, but it took this terrible experience to trigger it in me. If not for the bullying, I may never have developed an eating disorder or it might have come to me under different circumstances when I was older and had more ability to deal with it. I don't know. All I do know is that bullying can tear someone's life apart and make them excruciatingly ill. Mine is certainly a cautionary tale about the devastating impact it can have. It's also now, though, much to my own inspiration, a tale of hope. I have come through a survivor and am looking forward to leading a life not ruled by fear and intimidation but by self-love and dreams come true.

Kylie Rose's Recovery Tips

1. Be patient, gentle and kind to yourself. Recovery can be a tough journey with many bumps in the road. Healing is not an overnight process and one step at a time is all that is possible and needed.
2. Educate yourself about eating disorders. You will feel empowered if you equip yourself with accurate knowledge of what you are experiencing. You are the greatest expert of yourself, so ask what, how and why, so you can be armed with all the information you need to get well.
3. Separate the eating disorder from yourself. Learning to challenge and master its tricks and distortions is fundamental to beating it.
4. Listen to your intuition and honour yourself. Self-hatred and rejection is at the centre of an eating disorder, therefore recovery requires a large dose of self-love. Respect yourself by listening to your needs, as well as being open and accepting of your feelings.
5. Immerse yourself in your favourite pastimes. Spoil yourself, read a book, write in a journal, have a creative outlet, learn a new language, sit in the sunshine or volunteer. Whatever you like the most, do it!

Shining Spirit

Michelle's Story

Michelle's story brings to life the heartbreaking and devastating reality of what it is like to experience a binge eating disorder. After a journey filled with personal insights, acceptance and 'feeling feelings', Michelle is now at peace with not only food, but her body, including what she weighs and how she appears to others.

Growing up in Oregon on the west coast of the USA I was always surrounded by strong women. I had two amazing grandmothers, both of them perfectionists, hard workers, and known for making sacrifices for others. My parents divorced when I was four and my younger sister and I lived with our dad, seeing our mom on the weekends and holidays. Mom and Dad had a tense relationship for many years but are now good friends.

Throughout my childhood, especially after the divorce, food became my solace. Our family would bond over milkshakes and board games. Growing up, there wasn't much regulation about how much food or what type of food we ate, or portion sizes. I was always encouraged to eat everything on my plate. I think the sentiment may have been that my sister and I had gone through so much that the adults around us didn't want to step in and regulate any more of our lives. My biggest issue when I later developed my binge eating disorder was sugar and in particular ice-cream; when Mom and Dad were fighting, ice-cream felt like a retreat.

I overconsumed and comfort ate throughout my entire childhood, which resulted in me being obese. I became a social butterfly who flitted between the social groups in high school but was not really part of any group. I was known as being overly friendly and high achieving; that's how I survived. There was undoubtedly a mask with an intense desire to feel loved and wanted but while I was overweight as a child and early teen I honestly didn't care a great deal about how I looked. My take was: 'I'll do whatever I want, eat how I want, and those "skinny" girls have no idea what is beautiful'. I had removed myself from caring and was relatively happy, because I didn't feel any pressure to be thin.

When I was sixteen, my aunt lost weight on a diet that was all the rage at the time. I started to do it and had immediate success. I also enrolled in an aerobics class as a gym elective. When I started the diet, even though it may sound strange to others, I didn't have an intention to lose a lot of weight but it happened anyway. It was nice to shed some of the extra weight that I was carrying and to start adding exercise into my life, however, when I started to lose weight, I began to feel pressure to fit in with the 'skinny girls'. I was tired of being alone and, like so many teenage girls, I wanted a boyfriend.

I was on the diet for nearly four years, by which time I was in college. Despite being a lower weight than in my earlier teens I was still obese and I got to the point where, unlike in my early teen years, I was tired of being fat and single. I went on a formal diet program and lost more weight and began to receive a lot of attention.

My weight fluctuated small amounts in college but my focus and self-worth started to shift and align with losing weight and continuing to be a high-achieving student. What started out as an attempt to lose weight became an obsession with food, skipping dinners with friends and going jogging before the weigh-ins on the diet program. The weird thing was that this newfound lens I was seeing myself through didn't impact my self-esteem. To be totally honest, I was happy with the way I looked.

It was nice to go to stores and by normal sizes instead of plus-sized clothing. I remember when I bought women-sized jeans from The Gap for the first time and cried with happiness at the checkout on the way out. People started to tell me I looked great, which was the perfect thing for them to say to a dieter, and encouraged me to keep going. My attempt to lose weight slowly became the only thing I focused on.

After I graduated with a degree in education I moved across the country to teach at-risk boys in an inner city school. I went by myself and it was hell. I was overworked and underpaid and found it very hard to cope with no friendship base. I quickly found myself burned out and had made the decision to move home when I got a call from a friend who said there was a job available in Australia if I wanted it. I said yes and was off to Australia within four months of the phone call.

For the first two years in Australia I was OK with my weight. It went up and down but I was relatively content and the obsession, although there at times, wasn't my sole focus. My job was fun but incredibly exhausting, as it involved living with American study abroad students for four-month cycles. Thus, I never really made lasting friends. People were constantly coming and going from my life. At the tail end of my two years, I took on a full-time job for an Australian university, ended my time with the students, and moved out on my own. What I didn't have at the time was a good friendship group and I was scared of being lonely.

Then I met Gary.

I was instantly attracted to him. He was well travelled and considerably older than me. He was intelligent, witty, charming and sure of himself. At twenty-four I felt great and ready to be in a relationship. Gary and I dated for a few months until he told me he had two problems with our relationship: one was that I was still a virgin and we weren't having sex, the other was my weight. This blow came at a time when I felt I was in a transition in my life. I needed emotional support and to be loved and cared for and here he was hitting the major button of self-confidence and self-worth in my life. All the effort I had put into becoming healthier and skinnier wasn't enough. He tried to retract what he said by saying I was just big framed and tall and that he wasn't used to dating someone of my size. Although I was furious with him, I didn't want to be alone and I wanted to make my first relationship work. Instead of leaving, I decided to have sex with him, passively accepting what he said and ignoring the emotional pain it caused.

I then made it my mission to get thin. I needed to keep my man happy. Really, I didn't want to lose something that I had wanted for so long – a boyfriend. I decided to go back on the diet program to lose weight. Gary went away on a trip for five weeks and while he was gone I dieted to the extreme and increased my running. I quickly became a wild, starved, hormonal mess. I was obsessed with being thin and the numbers on the scale could not go down quickly enough for me. Previously when I had dieted and lost weight, I had never really hated my body or who I was. Now I did. I hated myself. I wanted to be thin. I wanted to be skinny. I wanted to be sexy and beautiful for him, but not for me. I was desperate for his approval.

I was now weighing myself multiple times a day. I was skipping meals but bingeing after I had weighed in for the week. It was my 'treat' for all of the emotional energy it took to obsess about my weight. Gary came back from his trip and I was excited to see him. I was not underweight, but certainly thinner than I had ever been and I couldn't wait to hear what he was going to say. The first thing he said to me was, 'Wow, you're looking skinny, Michelle.' I was validated but utterly miserable.

I was starving and constantly worried about what I looked like. Whenever Gary and I wouldn't have sex I would go into the bathroom and look at myself and cry, thinking it was because I was fat. He would say things like, 'I can feel your hip bones. I can really tell that you are finally getting skinny.' I put back on some of the weight I lost and decided to be incredibly diligent with my dieting. The fear of gaining weight while with Gary became my motivating factor. This dieting–binging cycle precipitated my binge eating disorder.

After I had lost more weight and had dated Gary for about five months, I went on a trip home for Christmas. When my family saw me they immediately told me I looked sick. I had starved my spirit away. Since Gary wasn't around I felt as though I had no accountability. I let go and binged throughout the nights I was home. All I talked about was my weight. My family were really worried about me, which I didn't understand. I wasn't underweight at all, but when someone is obsessed with food you don't have a spirit anymore. There is no glow in your eyes. No thirst for life. There is nothing exciting about you because you have given yourself over to something else.

I binged for two weeks while at home and then went on a trip to Japan to visit my uncle. I weighed myself when I was there and realised I had put on weight. Then I was hospitalised while there and almost needed bowel surgery. Being in hospital in Japan was traumatic and I was sicker and more trapped in a starving and bingeing cycle than ever before.

After my trip home, I realised that I wasn't in love with Gary. We sat on the couch and I said that I didn't think our relationship was going anywhere and it would be best to end it. Gary replied, 'Michelle, my biggest fear is that you will gain back all the weight you have lost.' I was devastated. There I was one week after being in hospital, at my lowest weight, with a man I had done everything I could to make happy. I had sacrificed everything that was special and important to me to ensure I was something he wanted.

Instead, the one thing I thought that I had done right, my weight, wasn't good enough for him. We ended our relationship for good. It was the beginning of my downward spiral.

I began to eat huge amounts of food consistently and would only exercise out of sheer guilt to try to burn off calories. Although Gary and I were officially broken up I remained in contact with him because I didn't want to be alone. I tried to tell him that what he told me really hurt, but he said, again, that I had misunderstood his words. I remained attached to him for about a year. Throughout this whole time I binged. For a year and a half I lived on my own, bingeing and gaining weight. I had a gaping crater in my life that I was trying to plug it with food. My perceived failure and lack of affection was so overwhelming that nothing would take away the anxiety and loneliness I felt, except the moments of bingeing. It was so entrenched in my whole life and I felt I couldn't deal with it.

After about nine months of what felt like a living hell I decided to go to East Timor for two weeks as a volunteer in a rural clinic. It was a very healing experience and I didn't diet while I was away, and – amazingly – didn't binge either. I just lived. I began to change a little and realised that there was something better out there than the life I was living. I was still bingeing after the trip but I knew I had to keep pushing through the pain of it all because I wanted freedom from it.

During this time, I was writing a blog that was initially Gary's idea. It was a way for me to help others lose weight through me sharing my weight-loss tips. It became much more than talking about weight loss, however; it really became my binge eating disorder journal. Through blogging, I was re-connected to a high school friend who one day wrote a post with a photo of herself stating all the things she hated about her body. I was really struck with how it made me feel and I started to genuinely wonder if there was any woman in the world who loved her body the way it was?

I posted a photo of my body in my knickers with everything that my body had done for me. I had the post on my desktop for two days and then I decided that I had to post it for everyone who was struggling as much as I was. It went viral and I realised how many women and men were suffering and didn't love themselves. It got picked up by some very popular bloggers and my blog gained popularity. I was still bingeing and wasn't recovered yet. I knew I wanted to be 'there' and love myself and I believed that I could get there, but emotionally I wasn't quite ready yet.

The turning point for me was when I decided to seek help and went to a counsellor after a year of trying to fix myself through pseudo-dieting and denial. In the first session, I got honest with everything and let out the pain, disappointment and secrets that I had been holding in for a lifetime. My counsellor provided a nurturing, honest and open space, which I really needed. I felt connected to someone who wasn't worried with what diagnosis I had. She just wanted me to find myself again.

I began to feel much better and started nursing school. I did OK until second semester when I moved back to living with students and began to bake for them. It was a trigger for me and because I was stressed from working and studying, I put some weight back on. I felt very uncomfortable and felt nothing was working even though I was trying to eat intuitively. I was petrified I was back where I'd started. I wrote about feeling guilty on my blog because I was preaching anti-dieting, pro-body-loving antics, but I wasn't following what I was saying. I wanted to be perfect for everyone who was reading it and to lose the weight I wanted to lose without dieting. I wanted to tell everyone I had recovered.

I finished the semester and was exhausted. I decided to stop over in New Zealand on my way back to America for a visit. I had not talked to Gary for a year when I got a message from him saying that he had heard I was in New Zealand. He was living in Auckland and he wanted to meet while I was there. I was now much heavier than when he had last seen me and I was petrified of what he was going to think of me. I still had a strong perfectionist drive about my weight and the only way to silence it had been to shove food into me. I met him and immediately wondered how I could ever have found him attractive. I realised I was finally over him. I knew now I was strong in who I was and what I stood for.

It wasn't a massive and sudden transformation for me. The trees did not part and God didn't wave at me knowingly, making everything perfect. It was a succession of things and small revelations that changed my life as a whole. During the depths of my bingeing, I was waiting for the 'aha' moment that some people speak of. Instead, it was a succession of small things that linked together to build a chain of change.

One of those links was after I had an amazing conversation with my cousin's wife, who had never struggled with her weight until after having her third child. She told me that she had thought about dieting but had chosen not to because she had three daughters and didn't want to pass any negative feelings or habits on to them. She was choosing not to raise her daughters in an environment where weight was the determinant of a day or one's worth. Instead, she focused on fostering a positive relationship with food and exercise. I then thought about how much my own thoughts of food, body and self-worth could be impacting those around me.

I have now become determined not to let my prior destructive eating and thought patterns into my current relationship. It is not fair, to me or my partner, for me to be obsessed with my body and bingeing. I have to admit that I have been incredibly scared about having children because I have felt that I wouldn't be able to raise them with a healthy relationship with food. But I'm no longer running from that. I'm dealing with it.

What changed for me was that I began to really *feel* my feelings. Counselling helped me to delineate and give words to how I was feeling, and gave me the ability to unpack it all; however, the next stage for me has been feeling my feelings right now. If I am sad, I'm learning how to be OK about letting myself cry. We shouldn't squash our anger and sadness down inside of ourselves, particularly if we are throwing food on top of it. I now realise that if I had allowed myself to feel devastated and sad after breaking up with Gary, the issues I experienced afterwards may not have been nearly as bad.

Sleep and regular exercise also helped me; that is exercise I want to do, not running because I was trying to lose weight. Prayer, mediation and memorising powerful sayings have also been helpful. I have had to learn how to feel happy as well, which is weird to say, because for so long I had forgotten what it felt like. The world is such a sparkly, amazing place when you look outside of the sad and feel glee as well. Recovery is a hard road and is different for all people, but I have no doubt it's worth it.

The biggest thing I am working on right now is making peace with food and my body. I am focusing on asking myself if I really want a certain food and if my stomach can deal with the consequences of eating it. If I do want it and feel certain I will be OK, I focus on eating it peacefully for no other reason than for the enjoyment of eating. I don't want to eat out of sadness, exhaustion, stress or boredom and am learning that I don't have to rebel against a diet or any success I have. It's just food. I don't want food to be an enemy, a punishment or a way to martyr myself. I want to be at peace with it.

I believe that what I have experienced is of growing concern in our culture. I know, of course, I am not the only person to have had an eating disorder, but the number of people who don't like their body, who diet, starve and have a tortured relationship with food, is increasing and it saddens me that it's reaching even younger audiences. I now feel like I have the ability to verbalise what so many people with binge eating disorder are going through but can't articulate. If that is the one thing that comes out of this whole situation for me, I am OK with that. Just helping one soul means, in a strange way, it will have been worth it.

I am now at the highest weight I have been in many years; however, I have had more compliments on how good I look in the last three months than ever before. This still makes me do a double-take, because for so long I thought the only way I would be complimented was if I was thin. What I am beginning to realise is that being thin isn't the only marker of beauty. In fact, a friend recently told me I look so much better as I am now: brighter, happier and with a glow.

I feel as if my spirit is shining, which is more important to me than anything. If it means that I stay at this weight forever then I am now OK and at peace with that. My weight is no longer worth sacrificing for my internal glow. It's definitely no longer as important as my spirit.

Michelle's Recovery Tips

1. If you are struggling with binge eating disorder it's OK. It's OK that you have this. It's OK that you feel the way you do. It's OK that you are bingeing. It's OK you have gained weight. Things will get better but it will take time.
2. Reach out and seek help as much as you can, even if it is just telling a friend to begin with. Telling someone what is really going on will help you come to terms with and face your problems.
3. You must accept and love yourself where you are right now before you can make any positive changes in your life. This is what it really means to be at peace with yourself, even if where you are is not exactly where you want to be. You have to

believe you are OK and a good person before any lasting effort can be made to improve your health.

4. On your path to getting well it is highly likely you are going to have days that are not great. Recovery is a journey that never goes in a straight line and it's OK to have setbacks.

5. Don't diet, no matter what your weight. It's irrelevant. Know that whatever you need to do for your health is not about your weight, it's about the intrinsic value you place on yourself as a person. It's about loving you.

Sporty Nice

Danni's Story

Being kind and giving to others are wonderful human qualities, but not when they come at our own expense. Danni's story is one of a highly empathetic young girl who felt the needs and pain of others so much that it transferred to her experiencing the pain of an eating disorder, including a serious concern with overexercising. A realisation of the need for self-love and care has seen Danni not only recover from her eating disorder but have a thriving career and personal life.

Even though I have spoken openly about my eating disorder for many years, I always experience doubt when I do. It stems from thinking my experience is not as serious as other stories I have heard. I realise now that this belief is just a tiny leftover from my thoughts growing up that everyone else's needs were more important than my own. I am very aware that everyone who has experienced an eating disorder knows that the pain is not something that can be measured or compared, and that every person's journey is important and real. That includes mine too.

I had a very blessed upbringing in Melbourne with loving parents, as the eldest of four siblings. Despite being surrounded by love, I remember having negative thoughts about myself from a young age but don't know why. When I was four, a family acquaintance complimented my sister about how pretty she was and how beautiful she would be when she grew up. I was standing right next to her and, while it sounds so trivial, that moment is burned in my memory, making me realise that even from that age I had a strong negativity filter and would give much more credence to anything negative or even neutral, rather than anything positive.

As a little girl and throughout my teenage years I was a people pleaser and wanted to be everyone's friend. I started writing a diary when I was eight but felt I couldn't be fully truthful in what I said. I would have hated Mum to read it and think I wasn't happy because I feared this would make her think she wasn't a good mum. I struggled to be totally honest with myself and to this day, I don't really know what I wanted to say. I just know I couldn't express what I was really feeling.

This is somewhat ironic as I have always had strong instincts and could feel what others around me were feeling. I was compassionate and nurturing to others and wanted to help and even rescue people around me. It might have seemed like a lovely thing to feel and do, but I became detached from my own needs as a result. Everyone else's happiness was more important than my own and I wanted things to be perfect for them. I felt anxious and tense if they weren't and it would make me want to search for ways to fix things, often thinking things such as, 'How can I help them?' or 'What do I need to do to fix this?'

While I enjoyed my time at primary school, secondary school wasn't so easy. My experience with puberty and adolescence was the reason for this. I went to a small Catholic girls' school and I remember feeling uncomfortable in my skin from my very first day there. Our summer uniform was light cream, which no one liked to wear, but for me it was not because of fashion but because I felt incredibly self-conscious wearing it. You could see the outline of our bras and I never wanted to take my jumper off for fear that people could see my changing shape. I felt like I was the only girl who was experiencing these feelings, as others around me didn't seem to be embarrassed at all. I don't remember there being a strong focus or discussion among my friends about the way we looked until later years, I just remember feeling really uncomfortable.

Looking back now, I believe I had a level of body dysmorphia as I genuinely believed I was much larger than I really was. My changing body seemed to create a huge shift in my thinking but I was a very good actor and no one knew about my lack of confidence or how I really felt. I was popular and always bubbly and was achieving good results at school. I was on the SRC (student representative council) and was sports captain and I was also doing really well in sport outside of school. But there was definitely an inner conflict and I would have hated if anyone had known what I was really feeling as I was meant to be the helper, not the person who needed help.

I had always been an athletic and sporty girl; a real Sporty Spice. I started playing basketball and tried many other sports, but eventually channelled my energy to netball, which I grew passionate about. As I developed my skills, I started to play at elite level in state squads and teams. I was always critical of my playing performances but was not overly obsessed about my fitness. When I was sixteen, as part of the state team's rigorous fitness testing, we got our skin folds tested and were weighed. The tests were carried out in the umpire's office and numbers called out to a fellow team member to record the skin fold results. If your folds were too high you were given a letter that was a referral to the dietician. You had to walk across two netball courts back to the rest of the group so everyone in the squad could see who received the letter and who didn't. Everyone compared themselves to one another.

I was given a letter and was mortified. A friend in the squad later told me everyone was shocked when they saw me with it and became worried about what it meant for them. I know reducing skin folds in sport is very logical, it's about getting leaner so we could move quicker and faster on the court, but the way it translated to me was so much more than that. I was too big. I was fat. I was not good enough.

I was placed on an eating plan that I wouldn't classify as being very restrictive or faddish, but I did have to reduce my food intake and increase the amount of training I was doing. Though I actually wasn't required to lose much weight at all, my level of discomfort in myself and my body increased and I now strongly believed that there was something wrong with me and I had to fix it. From then on if I didn't make a team, I believed it was because of my weight not because of poor performance or lack of skill. My relationship with food changed and I developed rules around what I could, couldn't, should and shouldn't eat. It was a gradual change, but it was the thinking behind my actions, more so than the actions at that time, that was the danger.

In my final year of school I had my first boyfriend, which evolved into a serious relationship. Sadly this was not a very good thing for my self-esteem. He became the most important thing in my world and naturally his happiness became my priority and focus. We were in love and, at this vulnerable time in my life, I lost myself further. My thinking became much more negative and I lost my concentration at school and was very disappointed with my final results. I wanted to do a human movement course but fell short of getting in by two marks. I got into a Bachelor of Health Promotion instead, but I hated it and university life. I became a completely different person: unmotivated, slack, disorganised; the opposite of how I'd always been, and this made me hate myself even more. I had come from a nurturing school and suddenly I found myself in a place where I felt no one knew I existed. There was also a real party culture that never interested me. I had no idea of who I was or what I wanted.

When I was nineteen, I had to have an ankle reconstruction and in that same year I lost both my grandparents within a week of one another. It was shattering to my family and we were rocked by grief and shock. It hurt so much to see my family in pain. I couldn't take any of the grief away, which made me so frustrated and angry at myself. I remember thinking that maybe if I hurt and punished myself it would take their pain away. This was a totally irrational thought but it seemed to me the only solution. The pain I was feeling watching my family suffer was too much to handle. We were experiencing a normal grieving process but it was one I couldn't cope with.

I dropped out of university and eating disorder behaviours began to take hold of me. I had naturally put on weight after my ankle surgery because I couldn't exercise as much, and when I weighed myself I was horrified by the number I saw. I immediately began to restrict my food and increase my exercise. I read magazines and absorbed food and diet tips and began reading labels and being obsessed with the fat content of food. I lost weight gradually and began purging by both vomiting and exercising furiously.

When my twenty-first birthday was approaching, I had been in the grips of the behaviours for over a year. I was getting positive reinforcement from my friends about my weight loss and this gave me a boost of confidence. If I ran into people who commented, I would say it was because I was training and playing lots of netball. I wore baggy clothing to hide my body and I made a deal with myself that things would go back to normal and I would stop thinking about food so much after my party. While at the party I thought about how I couldn't wait until the following day when I could eat cake and leftovers, but the cake eating never came. The following day I approached the leftover food with every intention to eat but I heard a loud voice inside my head say, 'You can't have that. You can't eat that.' As soon as I heard that voice, I realised I was in real trouble.

Mum had been picking up that things were not right with me and she had given me the name of a dietician who specialised in eating disorders. I thought it was ridiculous at the time, but I was now terribly depressed and so I knew I had to do something to help myself. I had decided that when I got down to a certain weight I would get help. I didn't weigh myself often as the scales terrified me, but now I had to because I had made this pact with myself. It was a stupid deal, but the only one I felt I could manage at the time. I reached that weight two months after my birthday and I remember getting off the scales and going straight to Mum so we could book in to see the dietician.

The dietician was amazing. She diagnosed me with an eating disorder and even though I knew I had a problem I was incredibly shocked driving home with Mum and I cried openly. I was so scared. I saw the dietician at varying levels of intensity over the next three years. She told me her aim was to keep me out of hospital, which I was in danger of if I didn't start to eat more and exercise less. She understood about the voice I was now hearing in my head all the time and the inner turmoil I was experiencing. She worked with me, and against my eating disorder, which made it easy for me to trust her and for my eating disorder to loathe her. I also saw other practitioners during this time, including a sport psychologist, psychologists, a psychiatrist, a hypnotherapist, a counsellor, a life coach and a meditation therapist, but I felt that none of them 'got it' and that they weren't listening to me. They didn't understand what I was going through as much as she did.

The dietician suggested I see a woman who had a daughter who was in recovery from anorexia. She explained the woman was informally counselling people, but she really understood the mindset and the dietician thought she could help me. The whole way to my first appointment I thought, 'Why is this woman seeing me? There are so many more people who are sicker than me who she should be seeing and I'm wasting her precious time. Other people should be seeing her before me.' My eating disorder voice was also incredibly strong, telling me it was going to be a waste of time.

When I arrived at the appointment the carer spoke straight to my heart and she immediately knew what I had been thinking, including all the thoughts I had about not being sick enough or good enough, or that her seeing me was wasting her time. Even though she wasn't a trained professional, I trusted her and saw her in tandem with the dietetic support for two years. I was diligent with attending appointments but, despite that, nothing was really changing for me and I wasn't getting well.

Initially, things got worse but there was something keeping me going. I met several other sufferers and wanted to save them. My dietician told me that I could help them one day but I needed to help myself first. I kept going because I thought I might have the capacity to help others. I believed when I was well I would be able to do some good from my experiences and that drove me forward, but it was clearly not the right motivating factor that supported me to get well.

My dietician called me out on the fact that I was listening to her but not making any changes. We went right back to basics with a simple meal plan and I finally decided to throw myself into recovery. In the first week I stuck to the meal plan religiously. I asked her to be honest with me and let me know if I had gained weight. When I put on weight after one week of doing everything I was supposed to, I cried almost nonstop for twenty-four hours, but the following day I woke up and did everything I was supposed to again and then again. I felt uncomfortable, I was scared, I was tired, but I did it anyway. I asked to stop being weighed as I felt that it was not helping me and slowly I retrained myself to eat. Unfortunately, while I was getting better with food, my exercise obsession worsened.

I was experiencing a lot of pain from excessive running and I went to have a bone scan, desperately hoping they would find a stress fracture and put me in plaster to stop me running. There was no fracture and I was devastated. By now I was obsessively running everywhere, even in my own bedroom, and I knew I needed a serious intervention. I had an addiction and felt that something drastic had to happen so that I could break it. After discussing my plan with my dietician, I went to the doctor who had performed my ankle reconstruction, who also knew I had an eating disorder, and I asked him to put my leg in plaster. I told him I knew it sounded ridiculous but that I needed a physical barrier to break my addiction, my mindset was too strong. I really felt it was the only solution.

He was initially shocked but agreed, and my leg was put in plaster for three weeks. The next three days were hell. I swam with the cast on and jumped up and down on a trampoline and my bed. I cried and was consumed with anxiety but I constantly kept telling myself it would get better. I had decided to do this so I had to stick it out. Slowly it worked and my exercise behaviours reduced and my recovery accelerated.

I started to see the dietician and carer less and eventually they told me they had taken me as far as they could. I immediately thought to myself that if this was recovery, I wasn't happy with it. I felt like there was something missing and that in particular I didn't have a great deal of confidence or belief in myself. I was functioning better but I wasn't really happy and certainly didn't love myself or my body. I was now nearly twenty-four and no longer playing netball. My captaincy of the team was removed from me the year before when it had become obvious I was sick and I was advised that it wasn't safe for me to be playing anymore. I had distanced myself from most of my friends.

I continued to be with my boyfriend throughout this time. I was assured we would get married when I recovered and this was a motivating factor for me. We did get married, but unfortunately, I went into it for the wrong reasons and we soon divorced. Even though the end of the marriage was an awful time, moving on from it was the best thing I could have done for myself. I was only staying in the relationship because I felt it was the right thing to do and I didn't want to hurt him or our families.

Mum and Dad were amazing and told me I could come home after my divorce. They encouraged me to socialise and start living. I had not really had a young person's life up to this point and I began to live more in the moment. I reconnected with old friends and made new ones, and had fun filling the gaps that my eating disorder had taken away. I felt I needed to relax and be more spontaneous with my life rather than being so rigid.

I saw some alternative healers and read books about inspirational people during this time but I found reading books about people with eating disorders incredibly unhelpful. I drew inspiration from other people's journeys in overcoming adversity, but in eating disorder books all I did was compare my illness to others. They always included weights and pictures of people when they were very sick and I felt like I just didn't measure up and it really affected my thinking. They made it hard for me to accept that I had an eating disorder and that I was worthy of help and being well.

I also started to do some eating disorder mentoring at a private clinic but I stopped because I felt like an imposter, knowing things were not quite right for me yet. I was proud of myself for doing so because it meant my self-awareness had grown. I later went back to it when I had a more solid foundation and I really enjoyed it, and I know that by being honest, I was helping people more. I focused on making myself more real. I no longer strived for perfection but for being authentic, which is how I live my life today.

After going out and having a great time, I felt confident and ready for a new relationship. I met someone who swept me off my feet and while it was thrilling and exciting to begin with, I soon found myself being manipulated. I lost myself again. My eating disorder never came back but my self-esteem and confidence, which I had worked so hard to build, slipped away. I was flabbergasted and angry that it could happen so quickly, and I was devastated that I had found myself in a similar position again. It took a long time – nearly a year and a half – but I eventually severed ties with him. He tried to keep me connected to him by playing on my insecurities but I knew I had to end things.

Recovering from that relationship was even harder than recovering from my marriage break-up because now I felt like I was tainted. I felt worthless and lost all over again. I had to rebuild and there were times when I exercised more than I should while trying to find myself again. Prior to the relationship, I had worked so hard to get myself to a positive place; I really didn't think it could be taken that quickly. It just demonstrated to me that recovery is a process and that I still had some work to do.

I knew how to manage myself better now and I kept on top of things and did not engage in eating disorder behaviours. I surrounded myself with positive people and used affirmations and listened to empowering music. I had done these things when unwell and I felt it was best for me to return to doing things I knew had worked for me. I also kept telling myself I had come through worse than this before and that I was going to be OK.

When I was with my ex-husband I had never given a great deal of thought to my own career. I believed after getting married we would have children and it would be my role to take care of them and him. When that didn't happen I had to re-evaluate everything. I had been working in sports administration since I left university, but now at twenty-five I wanted to branch out and find a career that really inspired me. I did think about counselling, but quickly realised that with my personality type I would want to rescue everyone and would have issues with boundaries. I decided I wanted to use exercise in a more positive way and to help others with that too, so I did a personal training course.

Considering my experience with exercise, my family were initially worried about this career path, so I sat on the idea for a while to ensure that I was entering into the industry for the right reasons and not so I could revisit my exercise issues. I loved the course and afterwards I worked in the industry and then got a job teaching the course. It helped me to realise that I was actually intelligent and that I had things to offer, which I had never thought before.

I started my own personal training business that had a very different focus to most others. I don't believe a client's weight or size is a measure of their success or health. My philosophy is to work with people in a way that is holistic and about their health and fitness, taking the emphasis off the strong culture we now have – that exercise is done chiefly to lose weight. I feel like I have found my place in helping others connect with exercise in a way that is about health and strength, not weight and appearance. I have always been passionate about self-esteem and body image as these things seemed to be the final piece of my recovery puzzle, and were things I incorporated into my personal training.

With my alternative approach to exercise and my passion for self-esteem and body image I contacted the Butterfly Foundation to see if there was anything I could do to help them. By total coincidence, they were advertising for a project officer to deliver body image and self-esteem education to young people in schools. I couldn't believe such an amazing opportunity had come to me when I got the job. It's an amazing role and I have since been promoted. My role includes working with young people, professionals, teachers and parents. I get to travel Australia promoting positive self-esteem and confidence. It's an incredible place for me to be and I continue to have my personal training business too. I like the balance they give me.

After my second relationship break-up, I felt it was best for me to be on my own and pour my energy into my work. I convinced myself that relationships were not a strength of mine, but that clearly wasn't a balanced way to think and I realised my reasons for not dating were negative ones. I began to date and put myself out there emotionally and I felt more empowered and assertive enough to respectfully tell guys that I no longer wanted to see them if I felt they weren't right for me. I was also much more resilient when people no longer wanted to see me.

I was logical about it and the experience of meeting people became a positive one. Previously I would have struggled to do that, but now I knew I needed to put me first. It didn't take me long to connect with someone amazing. I had actually known him for five years as an acquaintance and when he asked me out, things fell into place like they never had with anyone before. We are now married and have a beautiful baby girl and, with my new life roles as a wife and mum, I like and respect myself more now than I ever have before. I also appreciate, nurture and nourish my body even more so after pregnancy and have no interest in what it weighs post baby. I'm just so amazed at what it has done!

I still have a high degree of feeling and empathy for others, where I want to fix things and help them as much as I can. This is something I am always going to need to be mindful of, but in the past I felt that me not living was the thing that would fix those things for others. I now realise that was my eating disorder talking and that I can have good things and people in my life and that I am a good person. I give myself permission to live, and live well, now.

Learning to separate myself from my eating disorder was a key part of my recovery. I gave it a name and it became about separating me from it and realising it wasn't me. I called it Dug, which to me represented digging myself out of a hole. I had something to fight rather than fighting myself. My parents were also amazing. Dad bore the brunt of Dug but he always gave me unconditional love. Mum was very hands-on and drove me to sessions, explored treatments with me, cried with me and supported me. She was with me the whole way, which I am so grateful for. I also wrote positive affirmations all over my bedroom walls and I would read them every day. I avoided newspapers with stories that I knew might upset me. I know this was avoidance of a sort, but it was what I felt I needed to do to protect myself. I felt I had enough negativity inside my head and I didn't need any more.

I believe that full recovery can and does happen. That doesn't mean I don't have to self-manage; I do. I am sure other people who have recovered from an eating disorder do as well, which is absolutely normal and OK. But I believe every human being should manage themselves so that they can live their life to their full potential and not be held back by their own personality or their fears.

Now I manage me, not my eating disorder, and that is a sign that I am recovered and well. Recovery is what you want it to be. I know I will have life challenges ahead, just as everyone does, but I know I have positive ways to cope and deal with those experiences. I am not afraid of that now and am always looking for ways to build my resilience and confidence. I do it so I can not only deal with those situations when they arise, but be a stronger and happier person in general.

Danni's Recovery Tips

1. You can't get well until you are on your own side. You have to work to believe there is another way to live, and there absolutely is. Back yourself and believe you will recover. When that is hard, be guided by people you know are there to help you and trust in what they say to do – then do it. Recovery can be exciting.
2. Exercise is something we all should do for the benefits it brings to our mental and physical well-being, but it should not be torturous or compulsive. If overexercising is a part of your eating disorder, or even something you just do, please seek professional help.
3. Self-esteem and learning to love yourself will be the things that will see you recover and allow you to live a life that is fulfilled and happy. Do and surround yourself with things that help make you feel at your best and most confident.
4. Find ways to bring as much positivity into your life as possible. Learning positive affirmations,

getting together a collection of powerful quotes and reading inspirational books are all things you will likely find helpful and motivating.

5. As you enjoy life in or post recovery – because I know you will! – learn to find ways to bring exercise and movement into your life that are enjoyable and fun. Exercise should not have a weight focus, but be about you finding something that makes you feel alive and confident, filled with energy and joy.

Real Life

Elise's Story

Elise could be given any number of amazing personal compliments, but 'survivor' is surely the term that best describes her many years of experiencing anorexia, bulimia and depression. A shining light for anyone who believes recovery is not possible, even after multiple setbacks, Elise now lives in a world that is real, vibrant and filled with promise.

I was born and grew up near Mount Gambier in South Australia on a cattle farm with my older sister Heidi and fantastic parents. Growing up, I felt like I had a perfect life. Many of my extended family lived nearby and we were close knit. I was always surrounded by a real sense of community and had every level of love and support a girl could want. I also loved school and was very bright with a passion for reading.

Just before I started high school, Mum was diagnosed with aggressive breast cancer. Suddenly my perfect life was shattered. I didn't know where to turn or what to do. I wanted to cry when the diagnosis was confirmed but at the same time I didn't. I thought it was better to focus on not crying and being in control to preserve my emotions. Everyone reacted in their own way and I often felt like I was watching what was happening from afar. I was upset but did nothing to show it, keeping it all inside. Mum had to begin treatment almost immediately and my parents encouraged me to tell my friends what was happening. They all cried but I still didn't and they asked lots of questions that I didn't know how to answer. My diary from this time is very clinical and detached. It never contained any expression of sadness or fear, just the facts.

I started high school and in the first term, my home group teacher was very kind, saying she was there to support me. I didn't see the point in talking about my feelings, though, because I thought it wasn't going to change the situation. As people found out about Mum, they would often try to hug me, which I hated as it made me feel uncomfortable.

The day Mum was to have a mastectomy in Adelaide, five hours from home, was also the day of my tennis grand final. Mum and Dad wanted me to stay and play, which I did, and then travel up to see her the next day. When I arrived, Dad and Heidi were talking about how awful the previous day had been and I had no idea what to do or say. I suddenly felt like a burden and a pain. It was the beginning of me starting to think I couldn't do anything right and that I needed to fix myself to make things better.

I wanted to do more to help at home so I started to pack my own school lunch. It wasn't long before I began to lose weight, even though it was never my intention. I just wanted to be better and healthier and I began doing sit-ups so I could look good in bathers for when we went on a holiday later in the year. My aunty saw me doing the sit-ups one day and asked me what I was doing. I told her I wanted to have a flat stomach, which she reacted strongly to, telling me I didn't need to do them. This prompted me to start exercising in secret.

I was thrilled when we went shopping and I found a bikini I liked. When we went on the holiday it became clear I had lost weight because my clothes no longer fitted me. Mum asked me how much weight I had lost. I told her not much, but she said I should stop, which made me panic. I was pleased I had been losing weight – it made me stop feeling so helpless in regards to Mum's illness and instead allowed me to spend time concentrating on whether I had eaten right and done the exercise I needed to do. I was trying to forget one thing and focus on another. I was getting a high from losing weight and felt like I was finally doing something right.

I saw the school counsellor because my parents wanted me to and she advised I see a psychologist to help me sort through my feelings about Mum's illness. I hated going because I felt so exposed. I felt like I had failed and only saw her twice. I started to be more structured with the exercise I was doing and began to develop obsessive compulsive traits, which scared me. I would be swimming laps of the pool and feel like I could not stop, even if I wanted to. I had to keep going and going.

By now I had a voice inside my head that began to take hold of my thinking. My friends became worried about me. They told my previous home group teacher and she spoke to me, telling me I had anorexia. I found that incredibly presumptuous, especially as she went on to tell me why I didn't eat and for what reasons. She also said she had struggled with anorexia and regularly still did not eat during the day at school!

Looking back now, it was the worst thing that a figure of authority could have said to me. Immediately after we spoke I started to notice I had a lot of noise in my head that made it virtually impossible for me to concentrate on anything else. Later that day in front of a friend, the teacher approached me again, telling me she had rung my mum and told her I had anorexia. I was furious. I realise she had a duty of care but I felt she could have told me what she was going to do. I am sure Mum must have been devastated, especially after all she had been through, to hear this about me. I was dreading going home and over dinner that night, Mum told me she had been rung by the school. Mum asked me what I was eating and told me that I had lost too much weight and I had to eat more. The voice inside my head got incredibly loud, telling me I needed to be very, very careful.

I named the voice rex (rex never deserves to be capitalised like a real name) and he told me that if I shared too much they would stop me from losing weight and that I was nowhere near perfect enough yet. He told me everything in my life would fall apart and everything I had worked towards would end. I tried to reply that it wasn't true, but his voice was louder. After being made to eat dinner I felt an intense need to hurt myself. That night I bruised my arms and felt better. I had to pay for what I had eaten, rex said so.

The teacher started to give me twice-weekly counselling sessions. She was religious and tried to talk to me about God, which I couldn't relate to. During our conversations, rex was so loud it was nearly impossible to listen to her, but every time I tried to speak, she would just keep talking anyway. One day I didn't turn up to see her. When my friends found out they went to see the school counsellor, which made me extremely mad. My friends told me I was sick, which I thought was ridiculous. It was a hot day but I was freezing and was now having difficulty feeling my hands. The counsellor rang my parents and told them to take me to a doctor. I was referred to a Child and Adolescent Community Health Service psychologist and a community dietician, but it was going to be a while before I could get in to see them.

I was totally trapped now and felt I had to continue with my behaviours. I could no longer sleep well or for long periods of time because rex was never quiet. I went to the doctor, consumed by rex and absolutely petrified because rex told me that the doctor would weigh me and everyone would see I was overweight. My obsessive compulsive disorder was also very bad at this time, telling me things like if I ate with cutlery that had a pattern on it, the food would contain more calories and I would gain a huge amount of weight.

I had to wait two hours in the waiting room to see the doctor. The whole time rex screamed at me and I sat shivering with fear and cold. I told the doctor I didn't want to be weighed. She was quite old and seemed to have no idea what she was doing; she suggested a multivitamin might help. She took no other measure of my health. My parents had been relying on the doctor to confirm I was unwell but I was thrilled it never happened, making me think I was OK. I then went to see the dietician and psychologist. To begin with I was with my parents, who told them about my weight loss and irrational beliefs, but when they left and I was asked for my version I told the dietician and psychologist it was a very sad story but it wasn't me. I genuinely didn't believe it was. The psychologist asked me if I thought I had anorexia to which I said no, perhaps I just had 'issues with food'.

We started out doing cognitive behavioural therapy but it wasn't helpful. I knew that if I ate a piece of fruit I would not put on weight but rex's voice was so much louder than my own or anyone else's. He forbade me to talk about him to anyone. I was not allowed to utter his name. At thirteen years of age, I was completely under the control of rex and I did everything he said. I told the psychologist I wasn't allowed to talk to her but not why, which made her job very difficult. She recommended I see a visiting paediatric psychiatrist, who I hated from the moment we met.

He was not an eating disorders specialist and simply asked me what my friends were like and if they were dieting. He asked Mum about our family history but found no links to mental illness. He asked what scared her most about my illness and she said she was afraid I was going to die. I thought that was stupid because I believed I was making myself better by attempting to attain perfection. Mum began to cry because she could no longer see the daughter she had raised. I had become totally alien to her in the space of a few short months and she could see that rex was in complete control of me.

The appointment ended with the psychiatrist telling Mum we needed to spend quality family time together immediately after the session, something that did not happen. It was too painful for both of us. I had an appointment with the dietician that same afternoon. Upon seeing me, the dietician broke down and told me she didn't know what to do. She said she was happy to keep seeing me but that she felt powerless to help with my eating. I found out later that if I had let her weigh me that day I would have been admitted to hospital.

The day before my fourteenth birthday I was looking at photos of when I was younger and I realised how much easier and better my life had been then. I told my parents I was going to eat more, which made them happy but little did I know that despite making that decision, it was going to be very difficult to put into practice. Somewhere along the way I had made the decision to stop eating and now I believed it would be just as easy to start again. It wasn't.

Everyone around me was happy about my decision to eat more. The only person who was suspicious was my psychologist, who knew that there was more to it than that. I stopped being honest with her, wanting things to just be fixed and over with. I ate and hated feeling full but I kept going. I gained some weight over a few months but I wasn't happy with how I looked. I had phobias about certain foods. On a holiday to Europe with my parents, I didn't cope with the changing time zones, travel and new foods and lost weight again; in many ways it felt like I wasn't travelling the world with my parents, but with rex.

When I went to see my psychologist upon returning home, she could clearly see I had lost weight. In consultation with my dietician we tried a high-protein, high-energy diet but I was non-compliant because I simply didn't want to put on weight. That summer was a horrible one. I felt like I didn't have a moment's peace from rex and I didn't want to be around anyone. The beginning of the following year I got a stress fracture in my foot from excessive running. I was put on crutches and started to gain weight. Within a few months, I had put on enough weight to be physically stable again but I felt hideously uncomfortable.

I had been learning Japanese at school and had always had a fascination with the country because my grandmother is Japanese. I applied to go on an exchange there but when I went to the doctor to be medically assessed she told me I had to put on more weight before she would clear me to go. I did and then applied. Despite my weight gain, they said they couldn't accept me on the exchange because of my recent diagnosis of anorexia. Looking back, it was absolutely the right decision to make, but I was devastated. It was the reason I was trying to stay healthy and immediately afterwards I felt like the whole 'health' undertaking was not working. I began to restrict again.

By now both my psychologist and dietician were extremely frustrated and very scared. They felt out of their depth and had no choice but to refer me to a psychiatrist in Adelaide who was a specialist in eating disorders. My compulsiveness around exercise was at its worst at this time. I had to wake up at a certain minute and do calculated lots of exercise at exact times throughout the day. It was military precision and an awful way to live. I told Mum and Dad they could never tell anyone I had to go to Adelaide to see a psychiatrist. I was mortified to the point that I made them stay in a hotel rather than with family friends when we went.

On the morning of the appointment, we all felt like it was my last chance and didn't know what was going to happen to me if it didn't work. The psychiatrist asked me lots of questions and then called my parents in. It was amazing. He had the ability to explain exactly how I was feeling and what I needed to do to get well. I remember hearing him speak and being relieved that he knew why I was doing what I was doing, even more so than myself. He said he wanted to admit me to hospital. I was petrified but relieved at the same time. I finally allowed my parents to tell others I was sick, but the reality was that people already knew.

Being in hospital was the first time I met others with eating disorders. I had a wonderful roommate, Sam, who made me feel less alone, but I struggled terribly with anxiety and often shook uncontrollably. I was put on antidepressants to help with my compulsive behaviours and continued to have terrible difficulties sleeping. At the end of two weeks the staff recommended another six-week admission. I went home only because it was Christmas.

Just before going to hospital I had started to purge because I hated feeling full. It was another way I could hurt myself. I still didn't believe I deserved the nutrients I was getting or really understand why others were trying to save me. I lasted two days out of hospital without purging but it then became an enormous problem for me, quickly getting out of control.

I did the first week of year eleven before going into hospital again. The first four weeks of that admission were hell. I was on total bed rest and had to eat what to me was an extraordinary amount of food. But I soon realised I was surrounded by people who were trying to protect me from rex and for the last two weeks, I began to be integrated back into life. I was allowed to go home for a night but my parents, living so far away, could only come on weekends, making the ten-hour round trip in two days. There was a lovely nurse at the hospital who became my replacement family during the week.

I reached my target weight by the end of the hospitalisation but it was a rapid gain. I still hated feeling full and in particular looking at my stomach. I had a gap in my community treatment upon returning home because my psychologist was on maternity leave and my dietician had left the region. I gained more weight but continued to struggle with purging because I felt so uncomfortable in my body.

I finally went on exchange to Japan for three months. It was the most amazing experience of my life but I got salmonella food poisoning while there and became very sick. I was hospitalised and put on a drip and lost a lot of weight. It was enough to trigger rex again. Two days after arriving home I went into hospital for two weeks but I found that admission very tough. I was jetlagged and didn't have my family around me as they were overseas on a long-awaited holiday. I wasn't compliant and ended up losing rather than putting on weight.

When I went home things slowly evened out. I was eating OK but still struggling with ways to cope if I felt things didn't go well, such as not getting a perfect score on a test. I was still purging occasionally and I had no idea how dangerous it was to do until I tore my oesophagus. I called Mum to tell her what had happened and she was both cross and scared, telling me I had to go to the doctor. He told me I just had to be monitored and so I went home, but after that experience I really felt like I was going to die. There were very few times when I was sick that I realised my behaviours were dangerous, but this was absolutely one of those times.

My year twelve studies were incredibly important to me and I realised I had to get on top of things to do well. I started to do better, but a few months into the school year, my close friend and roommate from hospital, Sam, committed suicide. It was such a terrible thing to have to deal with. She was a brilliant and amazing person and I am still in contact with her parents today. At Sam's funeral, her mum told me that I had to get better. It was a wake-up call for me in the worst form. Sam's life should not have ended the way it did and I felt like I now needed to not only get well for me, but for her too. Every month on the anniversary of the day she died, I eat white chocolate (her favourite) and remember how special she was and the profound impact she had on my life.

I finished year twelve without any major incident, and I was so proud the day I got my results. I got into my first preference university course, psychology, and moved to Adelaide to live at a residential college. I met some amazing people who were inspiring and brilliant, and I loved my course. However, I struggled with so much change and I began purging again. I was threatened with hospital, which made me realise that I needed to get a better handle on my life. Still, it was one thing to say I wanted it and another for it to be a reality, and when both of my grandmothers became ill at the same time, I started restricting again.

It didn't take long before I crashed, and while I was at home the summer between my first and second years at university, I developed major depression. It was such a horrible experience; one I wouldn't wish on anyone. By the time I moved back to Adelaide to commence second year and was able to see my psychiatrist again, he had to drastically increase my medication. I could feel when it started working and, just before it did, I found a brilliant psychologist who helped me enormously.

The depression was compressing everything in my life but once it began to lift I became intensely driven to eat in a more balanced way. Despite this, my weight stayed the same, just below what was best. I made the decision to recommence seeing my dietician from hospital as an outpatient. We decided on a weight that was healthy for me and I worked towards that even though at times I still felt uncomfortable about feeling full. But willingly going to see a dietician, then willingly doing what I had to do to put on weight was a huge step for me. It proved I was now ready to do whatever it took to achieve physical and mental wellness.

Since I've reached my healthy weight I have remained well even though in the past year I have had a variety of illnesses, including chronic sinusitis, glandular fever, vocal nodules and seven bouts of tonsillitis. The fact that I could go through all that as well as other difficulties such as my grandmother getting sick again and not have them be a trigger, has proven to me that I am past feeling like eating disorder behaviours are my only way to cope. I think this is particularly the case because I was also able to cope with losing little bits of weight while sick, without letting it be the downwards spiral it would have previously.

One of the most wonderful things I have done recently has been to get the 'Chrysalis: Unravelling Anorexia' exhibition to my hometown. Chrysalis is a beautiful art exhibition about eating disorder recovery and it was also significant for me to be featured in media articles promoting the exhibition. I had tried to hide my mental illness for so long from the country town I lived in and finally speaking out about it felt like my journey had come full circle.

Life after anorexia has not been idealised or perfect, which I imagined it would be when I was ill and trying to grasp the idea of a real life. I have brilliant days. I have shocking days. I have normal days. And it is OK for me to show how I am every day because that is real life. It is normal and that to me means so much. I've gotten to experience so many 'firsts' over the past year – first real period, first time I allowed myself to cry or express emotion at a beautiful photo and sad TV show, and the first joke that was made about anorexia around the dinner table, to name just a few.

I have realised that I do not need the 'comfort' of an eating disorder in order to remain in the world. I can live a hell of a lot better without it than I ever did with it. Just realising that I can be independent and cope on my own, minus rex, has been huge. The past year has proven to me that I can get through difficulties without rex returning. This has really cemented the belief in me that I am going to be OK.

My family, some very caring teachers and my friends have been a key part of my recovery. I believe that as long as you know there is one person out there who believes in you and your ability to overcome the illness, it can be the thing that keeps you going. Discovering me, Elise, separate from rex, has also been amazing. I now know I love bright colours, drinking coffee, sunshine and meaningful conversations, as opposed to losing weight, being in control and exercising for hours.

I want my story to bring a sense of hope to others. For everyone struggling, please know that you were not born to have an eating disorder. No one chooses that life. I guarantee that if you get past this, this one bump in a whole lifetime, then every day afterwards will confirm why you fought so hard for your place in real life. I used to read things like that when I was ill, and believe me when I say I never thought I'd be the person saying them!

Having anorexia is like chasing a rainbow no one else can see. The chase is futile because anorexia's final goal, be it perfection, happiness or peace, keeps moving further away the harder you try to chase it and the sicker you get. However, life with anorexia for me contained none of the colour promised by that far-off rainbow. It was nothing but a cold black-and-white existence; a world of extremes where everything was too much or too little, all or none, life or death. Living that way was, on one hand, gloriously simple because real life to me seemed complicated and messy. But the one thing that kept me from staying in that simplified world was the thousands of colourful shades of real life, so much more beautiful and tangible than that eternally-elusive anorexia rainbow.

These colours found their way into my black-and-white existence and are part of what pulled me back into real life. I saw them as the promise of something better and brighter if only I was willing to lose my footing momentarily and leave behind the world I had been a part of for too long. I knew it was an act that would ensure I would not lose myself. So I jumped and embarked on the process of learning how to immerse myself in the real colours of life without drowning. I now live among these colours every single day. Living like this means not clinging to an illogical logic. It is doing what makes me happy, discovering my hopes, dreams, passions, likes and dislikes, and finally allowing myself to take up space in the real world.

Elise's Recovery Tips

1. You are so much more than an eating disorder. Find ways to separate the real you from the illness, because it is *absolutely not* who you are.
2. Set goals outside your eating disorder recovery wherever you can, such as catching up with a friend you haven't seen in a while. Doing these things will help you ease into real life again.
3. Develop a list of helpful distractions and soothing techniques to use when you are struggling. A lot of mine focus on physical sensations to distract from any mental struggle such as washing my

hands with nice-smelling soap, lying under a blanket, squeezing a pillow or hugging someone.

4. Cut size tags off clothes if they bother you. Do not let a piece of material dictate how you feel about yourself!

5. Hold on to the belief that nothing is devoid of hope and your experience is no exception. Even if you don't or can't believe it right now, hold on to hope. It can bring you through the darkest of times and make you believe recovery really is possible.

On My Side

Mitchell's Story

A desire to fit in with a popular group in school prompted Mitchell to become overly concerned with his body and what he was eating, leading to him developing anorexia. While his parents and an inspiring teacher supported him in his recovery, Mitchell proudly claims that it was his own decision to 'get behind' himself and give back to others that saw him get well.

Eating disorders have a very female face. Some may think that as a boy and teenager this would mean a harder road to recovery, but eating disorders are a traumatic and horrible experience for any person, regardless of their gender. I never felt unheard or poorly treated as a male with anorexia. I had a loving and supportive family and the professionals I came into contact with never questioned how sick I was or suggested that I couldn't have an eating disorder because I was a boy. Eating disorders do not discriminate and I'm certain more men are experiencing them than we know about. I think many men have confused relationships with food and their bodies and are likely suffering in silence. I know I certainly did.

Like many kids, I was a little anxious starting school. I was very close to Mum and would have preferred to spend the time with her, but I eventually found my feet and became a good student. Having my older twin brothers look out for me was a great help too. I always had nice friends but as I got older I longed to be part of the cool and popular group at school. To me they had it all: they were good looking, great at sport and admired by everyone. To become part of their group I started to get involved in more of the things they did, such as football. I never really enjoyed it but I liked that they started accepting me into their circle. It helped to grow my confidence and it felt good to be more recognised, but only for the briefest of times.

I didn't feel as if my self-esteem was particularly low prior to wanting to be their friend but the more I hung out with them, the more my self-worth fell away. After a few months I became the scapegoat of the group and they started to tease me and call me fat. I was a little bit chubby as a kid but never obese. It was just leftover baby fat and, prior to being teased, my body was never a concern to me. I only knew I was supposedly chubby because I heard it from that group. The teasing was instigated by the leader of the group and when he made jokes about me and others laughed, more would chime in. Having half-a-dozen people laughing at you is a horrible experience and not one I would wish on anyone. There were so many cruel jokes about me but there was one in particular I remember.

We were at a birthday party and went out in the street to play. A neighbourhood kid asked what we were doing and the group leader said we were going to have a pig on the spit and pointed at me. I felt my heart sink into my stomach and I wanted to die on the spot. The party was a sleepover and all I wanted to do was go home. That was the moment I knew I didn't want to be friends with them anymore.

That night greatly affected me and while I stayed the night, I cried a great deal the next day. By now I was ten years old and had learned a great deal about what real friends were. I immediately moved away from that group and got new friends, who were great. My confidence and self-esteem had taken a battering, though, and the foundations for my eating disorder had been laid.

After the party, despite moving away from the bullies, I desperately wanted to lose weight. I thought that if I was thin and more acceptable to others I could shield myself from any more teasing and maintain good friendships. I began to tell Mum that I didn't want to eat certain foods and I began to read food and nutrition labels, specifically seeking out fat grams. Despite knowing very little about what I was reading, all I saw was the word fat and fat, to me, was bad. I wanted nothing to do with anything that had fat in it.

I just wanted to fit in and even though I wasn't hanging out with them, those guys still ruled the playground so I felt it necessary to lose weight. I started running on Mum's treadmill at home, not obsessively but certainly regularly. Reducing my food intake and increasing my exercise went on for two years. My weight loss was very gradual and by the time I was twelve, Mum picked up that something wasn't right and took me to a doctor.

I loved the TV show *Buffy the Vampire Slayer* and I saw Sarah Michelle Gellar interviewed in a teen magazine in a story that included her height, weight and size. I related to Buffy as she was an outcast at school and dealt with demons and bullies. I thought she was a really strong and kick-ass character and when I read her weight I gave myself a target to be exactly the same. When I went to the doctor and he weighed and measured me, I was the same weight as Sarah Michelle but well and truly under what was seen to be healthy for a boy of my height. Despite that, I was happy to have reached my Buffy goal. My happiness didn't last for long, though, as I was threatened with hospital, the thought of which terrified me.

Throughout the whole time I was losing weight I was becoming increasingly sad and anxious about going to high school. I wasn't experiencing a terrible depression but I became withdrawn and very quiet. The beginning of my eating disorder was very physical and I had no idea what was happening to me. All I knew was that fat was seen as bad and thin was seen as good, and that was what I wanted. I did have an anorexic voice that would tell me I was fat, needed to exercise more and that no one would hang out with me if I wasn't thin. It wasn't completely controlling me but was certainly there and starting to get louder.

After I was diagnosed with anorexia, I think it shocked me into getting better. I had been a patient in hospital with pneumonia when I was younger and I hated it. I really had no idea what anorexia was and didn't even really think I had a problem. I thought I was just dieting. I went home from the doctor and immediately started to eat. I was worried about putting weight back on but eventually things settled and I began to eat normally.

I felt much better by the time I started high school. I had good friends and felt more comfortable with myself. By now the eating disorder voice had completely gone and my first three years of school were good. My parents divorced when I was in year nine, which was difficult, but I had known things were coming to an end between them. It was distressing for a while, especially when Dad moved out, and I did find the change hard to get used to. They remained great friends, though, and I saw them both regularly, and as a result, I felt like I had a fairly regular adolescence until I was sixteen.

At the beginning of year eleven, my second last year of high school, I started to become more aware of what I looked like again and wanted to feel and look good. I guess I was starting to grow into a man's body and I wanted to feel as good about myself as I possibly could. I was studying physical education and one day in class we measured our BMI, weight and body fat composition with callipers. As students we did the calliper pinch tests on one another and called out the numbers and results to a larger group. When it came to my turn, I was fixated on the calliper and what it was grabbing. I know now it was just grabbing skin but when I looked down all I could see was fat. It tipped my mind straight into a dark place and that desire to lose weight came back stronger than ever.

The eating disorder voice came back immediately but this time it was loud and with me all day, every day. It constantly told me I was worthless and pathetic. It was like a broken record inside my head or a devil on my shoulder yapping in my ear. I began a vicious starve, binge and purge cycle that took over my whole world. I felt guilty even drinking water and I began to lose weight quickly.

Everyone noticed how often I would cry at school and had withdrawn from those around me. The happy-go-lucky Mitchell who made others laugh was no longer, and now I would sit on my own at lunch and tune out the world by listening to my iPod. I was incredibly depressed. People around me were very kind and often asked me what was wrong, but I would push them away and say I was fine. My mum and brothers noticed the change in me too, but I totally shut them out.

One day at school I felt like I couldn't take it anymore, so I messaged my mum and told her I needed to talk. I told her everything and she was great. She rang the school and told them what was happening and soon everyone knew my anorexia had returned. Without me knowing, she also contacted a good friend of mine and asked him to watch out for me. By this time, I had started to rebel with a wilder group who smoked, drank and cut school. It never felt comfortable to me but at the same time I felt drawn to them.

I went back to the same doctor who had first diagnosed me. I was very dehydrated but didn't require hospitalisation. I was referred to a psychiatrist but had to wait three months to get in to see him. I was desperate and felt so drained and fed up with life that I knew I needed to see someone sooner. I got into a Child and Adolescent Mental Health Service and I began to see two psychologists a week. They were a team and I liked both of them. They made me feel really comfortable and I saw them intensively for two months. They helped me attack not myself but my eating disorder. They focused on my food intake and getting me to eat more, but they were incredibly supportive and encouraging in the way they went about it. They helped me form a team against my eating disorder, which I really needed.

My parents were also a part of that team and they had to take a more forceful role in getting me to eat. We had many fights, but they took charge of me getting well and it was a successful intervention. I hated it at the time and the eating disorder voice was screaming at me, but I slowly settled into eating more and stopping purging. The voice slowly quietened and by halfway through the year I was managing OK. I was wary that it was still there, but I had more will and energy to get back into life.

A few months later, the voice came back again. My brother went to the police academy and my other brother moved out with his wife. All the guys in my family had left and now it was just Mum and I, and I became concerned she would leave too. The voice descended on me again and I started cutting school. One day a teacher confronted me and asked why I was missing her classes. I burst into tears and told her my eating disorder was back and she became the most amazing source of support. I saw her weekly for a one-on-one chat and she even sourced nutrition plans and books to help me. She went way above what any other teacher normally would and she became an integral part of my recovery.

Talking to the teacher helped, but I was still very unwell. I was completely fed up with being sick and I realised there was no way I could fight this battle and get well if I wasn't on my own side. One night, I sat outside my house and I looked up at the incredibly starry sky. It was a turning point for me. I looked up at the beautiful stars and came to the realisation that I needed to back myself if I was ever going to get well. I went to my teacher and told her that I wanted to develop a self-esteem program to help younger students as I felt helping others would help me. She was fully supportive and encouraged me.

I wanted to make the program very personal, not just resources and information anyone could get from the internet. We worked together on it for five months, including right through the summer. I was incredibly passionate about what I was doing and being busy made the eating disorder voice die down, just as I hoped it would. Having a focus encouraged me to eat better and while I often struggled with thoughts at night, I was coping better.

The program was twelve weeks long and covered topics like bullying, self-esteem and grief and loss. We trained my friends as peer leaders and they delivered the program to students in year eight. We sought professional advice from a number of sources and we anonymously shared part of my journal, which I had started at the end of year eleven. The journaling process was incredibly helpful to me and I felt it allowed me to purge all my thoughts on paper rather than through my body. Creativity was incredibly helpful as a whole, and I wrote poems and songs as well during this time.

Delivering the program boosted my confidence and, as a result, I started to talk to the media and other outlets more about my story and experiences. I wanted my story to help others and encourage them to reach out for help. I loved doing it and the rest of my final year of school went well. Finding a passion and a project helped me get well. It drove my eating disorder voice and illness away. I backed myself for the first time in my life and the eating disorder simply couldn't thrive when I was creating something wonderful and being passionate about what I was doing.

I still do have moments of feeling down but I can recognise that now and know how to cope. There has been a lot of change in my life this year and change is still something I recognise I need time to get used to. Mum has a new partner and she has moved out of our family home and my brother has moved back in. I am in my first serious relationship and have both lost and gained friends. It seems like a lot to deal with sometimes, so I have to be gentle with myself.

Change is a trigger for me. I like things to be constant but I have to recognise that it's a part of life that things change and do not remain constant all the time. I know I worry too much sometimes and I often need to talk calmly to myself to feel settled. I do relaxing breathing techniques to help steady myself and I push back against that voice if I ever hear it. Sometimes it does pop up and say something like, 'Don't eat that', but I ignore it and eat what I want because I know it's more important for me to listen to my own voice. I also now know that what I look like is not as important as how happy I am.

I'm currently working for a telecommunications company in sales; it's not my dream career but I'm seeing it as a stepping stone. I want to go to university to study psychology as I think I have a real capacity to help people experiencing mental illness. Everyone has their own story but I feel like I can genuinely tell people who have been depressed or had an eating disorder that I can understand the depths of despair they may be feeling.

Although the teacher, my family, friends and the professionals I saw were incredibly helpful in my recovery journey, I believe the most important thing that helped me get well was me. I was the one who had to make the decision to support and back myself and never give up. I had to do the hard work to get well. Although it seemed so hard at the time, it makes me feel proud and empowered now that I did it. I am certain that if I can pull myself through an eating disorder, I can do anything. With my whole life ahead of me that's a great belief to have.

Mitchell's Recovery Tips

1. Recovery from an eating disorder will require you to make changes to your thinking and behaviour. You have to channel your strengths and efforts to get well and harness all the willpower you have to know that you don't need the eating disorder and you can live without it.

2. Don't be afraid to try different things to help you recover. If you know in your heart you're not connecting with a professional person, try someone

else. Even as part of the public system, you have choices. Recommendations from others who have had a similar need are a great place to start.

3. Use things like creativity to help express yourself and put on paper, or into musical notes, or on a canvas, what you might be struggling to say out loud. Having creative outlets can give you space to not only express all the negative feelings you may have but write down dreams and goals you have too.

4. Be prepared to have slip-ups on your recovery journey. This is OK – with every step, no matter if forwards or backwards, or up and down in the same place, you will learn more about yourself and how to better deal with things. Each step is a chance to learn, even if it is one that you might think is not taking you in the exact direction you want to go.

5. Experiencing an eating disorder can be like living with a demon, but it's important to never stop dreaming and believing that you will get well and do great things with your life. Be on your own side, not that of the eating disorder, and you will regain sight of yourself and the amazing person you were born to be.

Miss Butterfly

Jessica's Story

Jessica could be forgiven for thinking that with having had a congenital birth defect and later developing bulimia that both her body and mind had betrayed her. Bringing her bulimia into the open and powerful experiences in group therapy have seen Jessica not only recover but now be able to share her journey of mental illness at the height of her time as a swimmer on the Australian Paralympics Squad.

We all have things that make us unique and different and I am no exception. There are lots of things that make me me, one of which is that I have no left fore-arm due to a congenital defect I've had from birth, as well as scarring on my neck and chest due to burns I sustained as a toddler when I tipped boiling water on myself. I was born in Sydney, the only girl in my family with three younger brothers. I was a shy child and was teased in primary school because of my disability and scars. I did have friends but was never in the popular group. A few older kids looked out for me, probably because teachers asked them to, but I never felt I belonged and was always aware that I was different. My way of coping with the teasing was to shut it and others out.

Mum and Dad never wanted me to feel sorry for myself, but that meant I felt I could never tell them I was being teased. I thought I had to keep things to myself and if I stayed quiet, maybe the teasing would stop. I would have liked to have been able to come home and say, 'It was tough at school today', and receive comfort. The response I got instead was, 'You just have to deal with it. You can't feel sorry for yourself.' I wanted to be listened to and given a hug. Dad worked a lot and it seemed to me he was away a great deal, and Mum and I clashed and would fight on a daily basis.

We moved to Grafton on the north coast of New South Wales when I was eight. I hated my new school but when I was ten I took up swimming, which I grew to love. It was a sport where I could have my head under the water and not have to talk to anyone. It wasn't long before I showed talent – by the time I was twelve I was being selected for state teams and, in my first year of high school, a national team. At the local and state level I competed against able-bodied swimmers and at national level, other disabled athletes. It helped build my confidence enormously. For the first time, I felt like I was being recognised for something positive rather than something negative.

Unfortunately high school was even worse for me than primary school. I did have friends, but my shyness was acute. Little groups began to form and I didn't know where I fitted in. I kept mostly to myself. I started to rebel at home and school but swimming was my saving grace. I had always been a perfection-ist and wanted to do things to the absolute best of my ability, but I no longer felt this way about my school grades. I certainly didn't became a bad kid but I did tell my parents I hated them, and my brothers too. It was my immature way of venting.

When I was fourteen, I was selected to be on the Paralympic training squad for the Sydney Paralympics. For the months leading into the trials I was ranked third in Australia and sixth in the world in the one hundred metres butterfly. All I had to do was keep that place and I would be on the Paralympic team. It was a very exciting time, but while I swam a personal best on the day of my race at the trials, so too did a number of other swimmers. My ranking dropped to fourth and the team could only take the top three.

I was devastated. I didn't want anyone to see how upset I was so I bypassed the coaches and jumped straight into the warm-down pool, but had to stop swimming after a few metres to empty the tears from my goggles because I was crying so hard. I felt as though I had let everyone down. A few days before my race I had received encouraging notes from kids at school. I'm sure the teachers told them to write them but I didn't care – it meant so much to me that they had taken the time to write anything at all. When I didn't make the team I felt so ashamed and guilty and like I had let my whole school and town down. I felt like such a failure.

My family and I went to the Paralympics in Sydney to see my friends compete. When we went to watch the 100 metres butterfly I was so nervous and jealous. I couldn't believe it when the girl who had taken my spot on the team swam a time that was much slower than what I had swum at the trials. I wished she had performed brilliantly and when she didn't, I was furious at myself. I tried to tell my parents how I felt but they didn't want to listen, telling me to move on. I did move on, of course, but I still felt horrible.

The local debutante ball was fast approaching and I wanted to be in it because it was finally something to look forward to after the devastation of missing the team. I asked two friends, but both rejected me. I did end up going but only because my friends found someone to go with me. I felt pitied, humiliated and now trapped in my disability. I hated my life and, because I had stopped swimming for a few months, I had also put on weight. Eventually I did start to miss the pool, and it wasn't long before I was back training. My first commitment with the national team was a training camp, where a coach told me I was too heavy.

I told my friends I wanted to lose weight and one of them suggested I make myself sick. I tried but for weeks I couldn't do it, making me feel like even more of a failure. I was so angry with myself, not only was I now fat but I couldn't even manage a simple task like making myself sick. One day I finally managed to do it and then thought things would be easy for me and I could eat whatever I wanted without putting on weight. But while in the USA at a swim meet, some guy said to me, 'Nice face, shame about the body.' I came back to school more withdrawn than ever and was restricting and purging every day. I wouldn't eat at school but then arrive home and binge, later purging the food I ate.

For the first months no one noticed, but Mum became suspicious and sent me to a doctor. I knew my parents thought something was not right when the doctor asked me about my self-esteem and how school was: not the usual questions. No one had actually ever asked me that before. I was used to being shut down and told to get on with it. For the first time I felt as though someone was actually interested and concerned about me, so I did open up, telling her I wasn't happy with the way I looked and had been making myself sick. She diagnosed me with depression and bulimia and referred me to a psychologist, but I only went once as I felt like they didn't really listen and simply gave me text book answers.

Two weeks later I was competing at an interstate event and while I swam terribly, I met Tom, a disabled basketballer, who I felt an immediate attraction to. I had always told myself that I never wanted to be with someone who had a disability, believing that people would assume I couldn't do any better. That was ridiculous, of course, and the fact that Tom had his leg amputated as a child made no difference to me. I was honest with him about my depression and bulimia and he seemed to understand and made me feel safe.

Tom and I had a long-distance relationship throughout my last year of school. By now I hated living in Grafton and I wanted to move to Wollongong to be with him. That final year of school was torture. My moods were all over the place and I was a complete bitch to be around. All I wanted was to move. I was seventeen when Tom and I moved together and I started studying public health at university. It was a daunting experience to go to university as I still wasn't good around new people. I started swimming with a new squad but slowly my depression got worse. I was lonely and shy and threw myself into Tom's group of friends but had few of my own. My bulimia continued and after seven months of living together, I decided I no longer wanted to be in a relationship. I now realised I had to make more of an effort to live my own life. It was very hard, but I went to every one of my classes and swim sessions and felt I made more of an effort to make my own friends.

In the early stages after breaking up, Tom and I were still talking. One night, after I'd watched him play basketball, he invited me to a party, but I found it an awkward environment to be in. Tom began commenting about the 'hot' girls who had been at the game and I felt humiliated and belittled so I discretely went upstairs to the bathroom in the house we were at and began to cry.

I felt numb and, with no real thought to what I was doing, I started to hurt myself. When I began to feel pain I quickly snapped out of my trance. I was a mess, but after I had calmed down and was aware of what was going on I phoned my coach, who came to get me. Someone had also called my parents and Dad instantly made the ten-hour drive to see me. A few days later an intervention occurred with Tom, his mum and my dad. It didn't go well and I was furious and again felt betrayed and decided the best thing to do was to stop communicating with him and instead begin socialising more and make better friends. I began to feel more confident in myself.

However, after only six months apart, Tom and I decided to give our relationship another try and we moved back in together. We began training for the Athens Paralympics and both of us secured a place on the team. Our families travelled to see us compete and while Tom won a silver medal, I didn't swim well. I was devastated and knew it was due to my bulimia. I knew that nutrition was so important to my success but I was lying to those around me and myself. Physically I was doing everything right, but nutritionally I was a mess.

After Athens I was determined to focus my energy on the next Paralympics, in Beijing in 2008, and so was Tom. He got an offer to play a season of basketball in Europe and so we moved there for six months. It meant that I had to do my training on my own. Living in Europe sounded glamorous but we were in a very small village, which was incredibly isolating and lonely. I was on my own most weekends when Tom travelled with the team, further contributing to my loneliness. I began bingeing and purging worse than ever. The only help I had ever received with my eating disorder up to this time was not really a help at all because I never really wanted it and it was too sporadic. I had seen a psychologist occasionally in Wollongong but I didn't understand why he asked so many questions about my family. I didn't see how any of the therapy was benefiting me.

By now Tom and I were talking about getting married but he set the ultimatum that I had to get well or he wouldn't propose. I then decided I needed to change and look good for him. I also realised that training on my own in a different country wasn't what I wanted. I began to lose the love I once had for swimming, so I decided to stop. But I knew that

I needed to stay active and be careful not to put on weight. I took up running.

We returned to Australia for six months but went back to Europe when Tom was offered another contract. I felt very anxious being around new people again. I began to withdraw and would literally lock myself in our unit. As an outlet, I started to run furiously to lose weight. Tom and I were now engaged but I was terribly depressed and still deep in my eating disorder. It began to take a toll on our relationship and when my parents and brother came to visit us in Europe we had an emotional conversation where I expressed what I was feeling in a very angry way.

I spoke about how I felt as though I had a neglected upbringing; not literally, as I had everything material a girl could ask for, but that I felt Mum and Dad weren't there for me emotionally. Mum said she felt as though I blamed her for my burns and scars, which I told her was not true but that all I really wanted from her while growing up was affection. My brother Ben, who I barely spoke to in my last year at home, told me he had spent years defending me at school to the point where he was getting into physical fights with other students to protect me. It was a painful and confronting conversation but I now saw Ben in a new light, learning that he had been doing this for me. For the first time ever, I felt protected.

It was decided it was best for me to come home and get treatment. I hated who I had become. Tom was supportive, but stayed in Europe to see out the season. When I arrived home I was once again alone, which was not good for me. I was having outrageous binges but also restricting and exercising frantically as well.

I went to an eating disorder clinic in Wollongong but the waiting list was horrendous. I was referred to a counsellor who told me about an inpatient clinic in Sydney.

Now twenty-two, I felt it was my only option. As much as it was daunting, I knew I didn't want this life anymore. Before I went, I begged Mum to come and stay with me. I hadn't spent more than a week at a time with her since I left home five years earlier, so we both knew my request was serious. She took time off work to be with me, which I was so grateful for. We still fought but I loved having her there. I realised just how much I needed her.

Tom came home and after a few days together he drove me to the hospital in Sydney, where I stayed for five weeks. It was finally the real beginning of my recovery. I didn't know what to expect but I was told it was a facility for people with addictions and had a great reputation for helping people with eating disorders. I found myself in a room with a drug, alcohol and sex addict. Initially I believed everyone around me had problems but I didn't. I soon realised, though, that I very much *did* have a problem and needed help.

I quickly learned I had no positive ways of coping with my feelings about my disability, my burns, my family and even my day-to-day life that weren't related to food. It was my drug, my addiction. Food was my best friend and my worst enemy at the same time. Even though I was so alone, the bulimia was always there with me. I soon came to know that the people in the hospital around me had the same feelings regardless of the addiction or issue they were dealing with.

The group therapy sessions I had in the hospital were amazing. I felt much less alone in listening to others talk about the same feelings and emotions I had. At first I was taken aback, hearing what others had to say, but their stories and those sessions helped me so much. When I became emotional listening to others, I realised it was often because something they were saying resonated with something in my own life. I was also introduced to an Anorexics and Bulimics Anonymous support group, which I went to once a week while in the clinic. Again I felt a sense of relief and belonging when I met women there I could so strongly relate to. The issues we were dealing with were all connected to our feelings and emotions, and a lack of understanding and self-worth; they really had nothing to do with food. It was a safe and comfortable space and when I left the hospital I was put in touch with a counsellor and continued to go to the meetings.

The counsellor I was seeing used Gestalt therapy, which I related to well and helped me to develop new ways of looking at things in my life. If there was something that upset me, we looked at why I felt that way and what was it about that situation that I didn't like. The therapy constantly brought things back to me, which was helpful and necessary as I had been very good at blaming everyone else for things in my life. It helped me realise that *I* was in control of how I reacted to things, not others.

I had no eating disorder behaviours for nearly two months after I finished at the hospital. Things were good. Previously, I'd had no coping mechanisms to call upon in my day-to-day life but now I did. I was more in tune with my body and more aware of how

I was really feeling. Even though it was advised not to do anything that would bring great change soon after leaving the hospital, I graduated, bought a house with Tom and got married. I was applying the tools I had learned and trying to differentiate between what was normal stress to feel for what was happening in my life, and what were bulimic behaviours. An example was my wedding, where I had to work through wanting to look my best like any bride, but not doing anything so dramatic as to tip into a terrible relapse. This was extremely difficult and, in hindsight, it was probably the most stressful environment for me to be in throughout the early stages of my recovery.

I had to keep reminding myself that I had been given a second chance, and that Tom and I were about to start a new life together. Even though I felt much better, Tom didn't think that was the case. It was a stressful time leading into the wedding and he was away with basketball a lot. Despite feeling stronger, I still in many ways felt not good enough and I did relapse into past negative behaviours a few times. Still, we had a beautiful wedding and honeymoon and I was happier than I had been previously.

The months that followed our wedding were very busy. Tom was constantly away and I was now officially retired from swimming. Tom won a gold medal at the Beijing Paralympics and was offered a fantastic contract to relocate to Spain to play professional basketball. We moved there only eight months after our wedding. I thought going to Spain was a great thing for us and I was enjoying my time there but Tom's behaviour began to change. I backed away, thinking I had no right to be telling him what to do when I had such poor coping mechanisms in my own past, but then we started to fight a lot.

It was a stressful time and I was mindful of my triggers, knowing too well that situations like this would usually propel me into old coping behaviours. It had only been just over a year since I had left the clinic and there were certain high calorie foods I couldn't eat because they made me feel anxious. I was eating nutritionally and well, but felt I still had to control my intake of certain things to feel strong. I thought this was an OK stage for me to be at considering all I had been through and was still working on, but Tom didn't.

My brother Scott came to visit us in Spain and one night witnessed a terrible argument between Tom and me. Scott said he wanted me to leave and come home to Australia with him. I realised Scott was right; I needed to get out of the situation that I was in. I had become co-dependent and had lost myself in the relationship. The decision to leave left me feeling somewhat liberated and at peace.

I returned to Australia and lived with my parents for a month. My parents understood that my recovery process was going to be long and so they knew that I wouldn't be fully well after only a year since leaving the clinic. They were still scared, however, and they told me how they really didn't know what to expect when they picked me up from the airport. They had lots of questions as to why Scott and I had returned home. I think at first they were confused about things, as Mum told me I looked like my real self and that she had never seen me so vibrant and healthy. I felt that way too, which was somewhat ironic considering I had just left my relationship and my entire life behind.

It was incredibly stressful when Tom and I got divorced but also freeing as well. I am proud of myself that I never turned to punishing behaviours with food to cope with this chapter of my life. I moved to Brisbane and knew I could easily have relapsed but I didn't. I had to work hard to stay well but even when I gained weight, I still felt strong. I had never felt so hopeful and positive about the future. Don't get me wrong, I went through all the emotions that come with a divorce: sadness, anger, betrayal, humiliation, numbness, denial and, of course, complete isolation. In the past, all those feelings would have sent me into a total frenzy.

I lived in Brisbane for a year and began working using my health promotion degree. I met some wonderful new friends and became much more social and fun. There were times when I felt so happy it made me quite emotional. For the first time in a long time I felt optimistic and excited about my future. I wasn't scared about things anymore, as I had been for so long when bulimic.

I decided it would be good for me to go back to New South Wales to spend more time with my family. I thought it was time to try to close the wide gap that had been wedged between us, so I moved to Newcastle where my mum and brother were. The initial months being closer to family were difficult, but now we are getting along well. My relationship with Mum in particular is better than ever and this is something I am incredibly proud of.

I started exercising again, which I am also enjoying. I did have to think carefully about easing back into it though as exercise can be a trigger for me – I needed to be involved with a sport that was fun. After all the years of using exercise as punishment it was now time for me to do it because I enjoy it. I started training with a triathlon group and I have met some great people and I absolutely love the fun and healthy environment.

I am now telling my eating disorder story and sharing it at community events and in schools. People had always told me I had a story to share, which I never really believed, but I now know that if sharing my story helps just one person, then it is worth it. Sharing my life and being honest about myself helps me too. The feedback I have gotten is so great that I know I am doing something positive.

I was always looking for a quick fix when I was sick but I know it was about me needing to look deep inside myself and change my thinking. For so long I had told myself I was unworthy and not good enough. I have now learned to say the exact opposite to myself and have learned to respect myself. Identifying my eating disorder as an addiction helped me enormously. It has enabled me to understand why I reached out for food in the way I did, and brought about a self-awareness that allows me to accept myself and realise that food was really not my problem – it was all my underlying emotions that I didn't know how to deal with.

The group therapy was also amazing as for the first time I didn't feel so lonely or alone. Others reached out to share of themselves to help me and now I do the same. It's really a full-circle experience that has helped me grow and believe I now have something to offer not only myself, but many others too.

Jessica's Recovery Tips

1. Be hopeful and persistent. Anything, including recovery, is possible when you have hope.
2. All journeys require you to take one step and one day at a time. Don't place too much pressure on yourself to try to race ahead with your recovery. Be patient and gentle with yourself.
3. Learn what your triggers are and why you have them in the first place. This will see you develop new and positive ways to manage stressful situations, events or people in your day-to-day life.
4. Different forms of professional help work for different people. Don't give up if you don't find someone or something straight away. There is a treatment out there for you that will help.
5. Surround yourself with positive people who are honest with you, but also make you feel safe. They can make an enormous difference in your recovery journey and indeed your life.

Somebody to Love

Kirsty's Story

The world of beauty pageants and international modelling saw Kirsty become so worried about her weight and appearance that she developed anorexia. Her illness went undetected in the world of modelling and was, to an extent, even supported by it. Now forging a path outside the rigours of modelling, Kirsty's story is one of learning to open up and express her true feelings, which prompted the self-care and self-love she needed to be well.

I know that many children have memories of kisses, cuddles and feeling adored by their parents, but that was not my experience of childhood growing up near a small country town in Scotland. While I know my parents loved my brothers and sisters and me, I came to realise as I was growing up that they showed this love differently to the ways other children received affection. I certainly loved them too and while I did get the occasional cuddle, it was a rare occurrence. I wanted it to be something I got all the time.

I got along well with my parents but did start to notice that my mum was different to other mums when

I started to go through puberty. When my body began to change I had no idea what was happening to me. No one had ever told me about what was going to happen, including that I would get my period. I panicked when it came and didn't feel as if I could tell anyone.

Mum eventually found out, of course, and got me the sanitary items I needed, but she still never spoke about it to me. She left them in my room for me to work out how to use them. I felt confused and more than a little freaked out, but despite not understanding what my body was going through, I didn't feel negative about it or the way I looked. I loved taking dance classes and using my body to move and have fun, and I think I dealt with it quite well, especially for a child who never had anything about puberty explained to her.

When I started going to a local public high school, being around so many new people soon made me realise what little affection was shown in my family and how different I was from them. I was very open with my feelings and they weren't. I wanted to be shown love and affection like I saw my friends getting, but I never was. I became desperate for affection as I got older and found it very hard that there seemed to be nothing I could do to get it. I wanted to hear someone tell me that they loved me and I became increasingly lonely in my own family, feeling more and more like an outsider.

It's not surprising, with my increasing need for love, that when I got my first boyfriend at fifteen, he was four years older than I was. Andrew was charming and seductive and he gave me what I so desperately wanted: love and affection. My parents never liked him, finding him overly confident and confronting, and they only put up with him because they knew I wanted to be with him. They hated the thought of me going out with someone who was so much older, but we managed to sustain our relationship for three years. He was by no means a perfect boyfriend and cheated on me a number of times. Friendships also became difficult. Other girls all had boyfriends their own age and my friendships drifted as I found myself spending more and more time with Andrew.

From my mid to late teens, my mum strongly encouraged me to become a model by entering my photo into modelling competitions and sending it to different agencies. I never won any competitions but came close a few times. I got an agent in Glasgow at seventeen and while it took a while to build up, I eventually got a lot of work. It was never really something I chose for myself though and soon the image- and body-obsessed world of modelling saw me turn from being a relatively confident teenager into a young woman with raging insecurities and body issues.

Despite the fact that my agency and casters were fine with my body, I quickly started to turn on myself and became worried about my appearance. I became self-conscious about my body and started to reduce the amount I was eating. I didn't want to lose weight initially, but sustain the body shape I had so I would continue to get work. Clearly, with still some growing to do, this was always going to be impossible. I believed I would get more work if I was thinner and all the models I was working with were obsessed with weight loss and their bodies too. There was constant talk about diets and new ways to lose weight. I managed to hide how little I was eating so others around me never knew. I was incredibly self-conscious and deprived myself of so many foods even though I was often very hungry.

I left school just prior to the beginning of my last year to study beauty therapy. I was seventeen, and after I finished I was offered a job at the school salon. I only worked there for a few months because it wasn't very stimulating. This was also the time I made the decision to end my relationship with Andrew, after discovering he'd been unfaithful. I was broken-hearted but decided to throw myself into studying my dancing further and being a teacher. I taught tap, jazz, disco and street dance until I was twenty-one and I really enjoyed it.

While I enjoyed teaching dance during this time, modelling was something else entirely. I think the only reason I continued was because Mum really wanted me to. I also started entering beauty pageants, including Miss Scotland. Beauty pageants were a pressure pit of negative body image, body obsession and diet talk, and I found every pageant I entered to be a terrible experience. I would never recommend anyone enter a pageant but at the time I thought it was a chance to help me get somewhere and take me further than the horizons of Kinross. While I did well and finished more than once in the top three, I never won.

When I was twenty-one, my family went on a trip to New Zealand, where my sister got married. On the way home we stopped over in Singapore and I fell in love with the city. A modelling friend was living there and she invited me to come back for a holiday. While I was visiting her I decided to see if I could get an agent. By now I was very keen to leave home as I felt hugely suffocated in the small town environment and I saw modelling in Singapore as a great opportunity. I returned to Scotland for two weeks and then moved. My parents thought I would only be gone for a few months, but I knew in my heart it was going to be much longer than that.

I loved living in Singapore; I was free and independent and loved being away from home. The only problem was I hated modelling. Modelling in Singapore was worse than Scotland had ever been as from my very first job I was told to lose weight and colour my hair. Initially I resisted but the constant pressure got to me and I became obsessed with losing weight. I ate only tiny amounts of food and would walk for hours in the intense humid heat. No matter how much weight I lost I still felt too big, and began to lose touch with what size I really was.

I quickly slipped into a depression, my entire mind consumed with searching for ways to lose weight. Being surrounded by advertising for slimming teas and detox programs did not help and, within months of leaving home, modelling had become a nightmare for me. All the Anglo-Saxon models were told to lose weight, likely because the Eastern European models were so much thinner than we were. I remember sitting in castings and hearing only tummies rumbling. We all knew it was happening but chose to ignore it either out of embarrassment or the realisation that it was a side effect of what we had to do to get work. I know without question now that I was not the only young woman who was sick with depression, anxiety and an eating disorder. Such illnesses were rife within the industry.

As I was only in Singapore on a holiday visa, things became difficult for me to stay. I didn't want to go back to Scotland so decided to go to Sydney in Australia, which was somewhere I always wanted to visit. At this stage I had no idea I was sick, even though I undoubtedly had anorexia. I got an agent in Sydney where I thought things would be better, but once again found myself in an environment where everyone around me was highly critical of my weight and shape. I was very thin and they validated this by telling me I looked great, despite the fact I was clearly underweight. I got a lot of work but the constant scrutiny of my body fed my insecurities. Where was the glamorous life of a successful model? It was certainly nowhere I was.

By now I had a strong anorexic voice inside my head and thoughts telling me I could never exercise enough or eat too little. I believed if I lost more weight I would get more work, but also that I would get a boyfriend too. I was lonely and felt I needed someone to take care of and love me. I did love being in Sydney, however, and I made some great friends. It was such a beautiful city and I got a part-time job in a restaurant, which I enjoyed. This made things bearable, but the modelling still made me miserable.

I started to avoid doing things so I wouldn't have to eat or drink in front of others. I began to isolate myself and started getting sicker. When my parents came to visit me they saw how much weight I had lost and commented on it but never asked me what was wrong. They stayed for a month and I felt they were watching me the whole time, making me feel more scrutinised.

When I was twenty-two, I met someone – Mark was very health and body conscious and strict with what he ate. I immediately felt there was no way I could eat more than he did and it made me even more conscious of what I was eating. I had longed for a partner and I did get some love initially, but then it was like being with my family again as Mark slowly withdrew and barely communicated. Things were OK between us for a year-and-a-half but I found myself entangled in a terrible relationship I didn't have the strength to get out of.

Mark got into a course in Melbourne and I followed him there. My eating disorder was worse than ever. I was extremely restrictive, would only eat certain things and barely ate in front of others. I continued to isolate myself from everyone around me, intensifying the feelings of loneliness I was already dealing with. By now I thought that maybe I had an issue I had to deal with, but I kept suppressing it. When you are receiving validation for how you look on one hand but thinking there may be a problem on the other, the validation is likely to win out every time because it's so much easier to believe.

Only my best friend, Lauren, who was also a model, thought that maybe there was a problem, likely because she had the same concerns for herself. I didn't have a good doctor and I genuinely didn't know where to start to ask for help. Even though I thought it would be a good idea to talk to someone, I never followed through because I thought I was not sick enough. By now thoughts about food and my body consumed me. Every minute I was awake I would think about food, what I was going to eat, where I was going to eat. I would dream and have nightmares about food too. It was the entire focus of my life. I had now been having thoughts like this for nearly eight years, albeit at different intensity levels.

I didn't know what I wanted to do with my life so it felt natural to follow Mark to Melbourne, where I found living very hard. We initially lived with his cousin but I began to have panic attacks about the type of food they were eating. We moved to our own apartment, which I chose, but from the first day Mark hated it. I took it as a personal affront and my self-esteem and confidence plummeted.

By now I had given up modelling. I had been working for a wine company in Sydney and I started to look for work in Melbourne but found it hard to get anything. I felt very unsettled and returned home to Scotland for a visit. My family were very worried when they saw how much weight I had lost. They commented on it but never asked me if there was anything wrong – something I was desperate for someone to do. I was screaming inside and desperately needed someone to hug me and help me.

Mark's life in Melbourne was going well but mine was not. I had no friends and I became increasingly depressed. I was achingly lonely and isolated and started to feel trapped by my own thoughts and feelings. I asked Mark if he thought I should get help and he told me I was the only person who could help me. I became sicker and sicker with constant feelings of not being enough.

By now I was barely eating enough to survive. I no longer had to be thin to model, but that was irrelevant now. I was totally gripped by the eating disorder. Mark's mother came to visit for a month and I ended up spending a great deal of time with her. Ironically, she recognised I was very unhappy and encouraged me to leave him, but soon my ability to do that was taken away from me as Mark broke up with me. I was distraught, having no idea what was to become of me. I had to move out, even though I had found our apartment.

I came to the realisation I couldn't live the way I was anymore. I had been emailing a friend who was being incredibly supportive and telling me to reach out for help. I rang a helpline but found them useless. I felt they simply fobbed me off to go and see a doctor but I didn't have one nor had any idea of how to go about finding the right one for me. A dear friend told me about her doctor and encouraged me to see her. I was petrified sitting in the doctor's waiting room and I wanted to leave every second I was there. I had no idea what I was going to say but I told her I thought I may have an eating disorder and that I was depressed. From there she took control and led me through the conversation. She weighed and measured me and told me that I was unwell and needed psychological help.

She referred me to a psychologist, which I initially found very hard. Growing up in such a closed family it was difficult to express my thoughts and feelings, but from the first appointment I knew it was where I needed to be. It was helpful to talk about my upbringing and how it was affecting the way I thought and expressed myself. It made me realise and learn so much about myself as a person, and I finally found, with the psychologist and the doctor, I had a support system. I saw the psychologist intensively for nearly six months and I still see her on an irregular basis now. She has helped me to express, rather than repress, my feelings. When I'm not happy with something I can now look at it differently and try to work out why I'm feeling that way and how I can think and deal with it more positively.

I slowly began to put on weight and I started a business with a friend, an online wine store. I am enjoying it, but will admit to still not being fully certain about what I want to do with my life. Wine is again something I feel I have fallen into and not really chosen. Once I started to feel better I did want to get back into modelling. I went to a lot of different agencies but none wanted me, which I couldn't understand. Initially I found it very hard, as even though I never really enjoyed modelling, it paid well and was really all I knew. It did cross my mind that the reason I was not getting offered work was because I had put on weight, but with the support I was receiving I came to realise that I needed to close that chapter in my life and leave modelling behind. I realised that there was little chance of a long-term career for me and it had never made me happy. Truthfully, it had made me miserable.

I lived on my own for a long time and I loved it. It was so wonderful to have my own space both metaphorically and physically. It was the first time in my life I really concentrated on me and what I need to be happy and I had everything set up the way I wanted. It was my space and it finally felt like I was living my own life. I developed a close circle of friends and I believe all that self-nurturing led me to a wonderful new relationship. I now live in Perth and it's amazing here, I feel like I can love myself and someone else in a way that is truly real.

I told my parents about my eating disorder via a letter about three months after I starting seeing the psychologist. I knew this was the best way to communicate with them about it. I'm sure the truth was just too difficult to bear and would have broken Mum's heart. She has never spoken about my eating disorder openly and I highly doubt she, or anyone else in my family, ever will. I can see in her letters it is very hard and awkward for her to talk about. She is being supportive, but in her own way.

I now feel so much stronger within myself. I know that I won't settle for less than what I deserve in a relationship and I like myself now. I know what I need and what I want, but of course I'm still a work in progress. The best thing I ever did for myself was stop modelling. It was such a toxic environment.

Getting professional help was also clearly a turning point, as it has taught me to be kinder to myself and not be afraid of getting in touch with what I truly feel and want. I needed support and to have someone help me learn to trust and talk about my feelings, which I now do. I have never had role models in my life who have encouraged me to be expressive and open. I am that role model for myself now and I'm proud of the job I am doing in creating a more open and accepting me.

Kirsty's Recovery Tips

1. Try not to be afraid of what you are feeling. Talking to someone you trust, whether a friend or a professional, will help you to get in touch with what you not only feel, but need. This will be the beginning of your path to recovery.

2. Don't hide yourself away from others. Eating disorders thrive on isolation but people don't. We especially need caring and loving people around us when we are unwell. Accept the help others give you, or reach out as hard and as long as you can to get the support you need.

3. Don't compare the way you look to models or indeed anyone. Our society places far too much emphasis on thinness and external appearances, and being thin or a model is not a guarantee of happiness. It is also not the glamorous and fun profession that many think it is.

4. Having an eating disorder can feel like your whole mind is consumed with negativity. Focusing on positive things is hard to do, but learning a practice like meditation can help both retrain your thinking and quieten that voice inside your head that is keeping you unwell.

5. Reading books about eating disorder recovery and also stories of love, hope and relationships helped me immensely. Reading such things can help you realise you are not alone and that others may have similar feelings and emotions. Reading inspiring things can also be a beautiful and reflective time for you to set aside to relax and unwind.

Taking Flight

Emma Kate's Story

An incredibly bright and high-achieving girl, Emma Kate's anorexia began in very physical terms, staying with her throughout most of her teenage years. During her journey of recovery through at-home and inpatient treatment, Emma Kate's lifeline was her passion for making beautiful things and expressing her creativity. Hers is a story that shows healing and treatment can come in many forms.

I was a go-getter as a little girl – bright, loving and involved in lots of extracurricular activities. I took dance, piano, violin, swimming, tennis, orienteering and art classes and I loved them all. My parents were encouraging, loved me unconditionally and never pushed me to do anything I didn't want to do. As the only child of their marriage, I grew up spending a lot of time with older people. I loved to talk with adults and was often referred to as an old soul.

I loved going to primary school in Adelaide, where I had a wide circle of friends and fantastic teachers. As an absolute perfectionist, school work was extremely important to me and I always felt an unquenchable drive to do far more than was expected of me. If I was asked to do up to page twenty for homework, I would go to page twenty-six; it was just my nature. Mum has told me that even in kindergarten, where other children would constantly move from one activity to the next, I would stay focused and determined to completely master one activity before moving on, even if it meant being on my own.

I was a relatively healthy child but had a variety of dental problems from a young age that required numerous operations. This made me quite phobic about the dentist and when, aged eleven, I needed to have four teeth removed in preparation for braces, I was terrified. In the days following the operation my healing mouth made it physically impossible to eat and I quickly lost the appetite for food. By the time my mouth had healed, I had lost all desire to eat and my normal appetite never returned.

While my friends were growing up quickly, I had not started puberty. Although I was conscious of it, body image was never a factor in my eating disorder and I certainly never felt a desire to lose weight. But as my apathy towards food heightened and I began to lose weight, people around me became concerned. Mum took me to our local doctor and I was referred to a paediatrician, who weighed and measured me before explaining that I was fine and just going through a phase before puberty. Mum never felt comfortable with this conclusion and, soon after, we returned to the doctor to get an alternative referral.

By now, other worrying symptoms were becoming apparent, including having consistently purple hands due to bad circulation and extreme sensitivity to the cold. The second paediatrician's diagnosis was entirely different and I was told sternly, 'You have the body of an anorexic but not the mind of one. If you don't put on weight I will admit you to hospital.' I was terrified of the doctor and his strict instructions. I wanted to obey him but felt incredibly helpless. Eating no longer felt like a choice. My ability to think clearly had vanished and the tiniest quantities of food made me feel uncomfortable and full. I was so naive to this new world and had no idea what anorexia was.

When I returned to the paediatrician and had not gained weight, I was immediately admitted to hospital. I was considered so medically compromised and unstable that I wasn't allowed to go home to pack clothes. Within hours, I'd had a nasogastric tube inserted and was kept on strict bed rest. Earlier that week I had been attending school, walking to and from appointments, and had even competed in an orienteering championship. In stark contrast, I was now bedridden, had a tube in my nose, constant medical observations and was not allowed even to walk to the shower.

I spent ten weeks in the adolescent ward of the hospital. Once a week, I saw a counsellor and dietician, which was not nearly enough support for the emotional trauma I was experiencing. For the first month, I was tube fed twenty-four hours a day. Gradually, the hours of feeding were reduced so I could have the chance to eat meals. After six weeks, I was granted weekend leave as an experiment to test how I would cope in the real world. It was frightening to return to food again after a month of not eating. Eating with the tube obstructing my throat was difficult and painful.

While the nasogastric feeding had been necessary for my survival, it was largely a Band-Aid measure.

The first few weeks in hospital I felt terribly homesick. I was scared and wanted nothing more than to be back at school like a normal twelve-year-old. One day, however, this feeling changed. There was a moment in hospital when I had a realisation: whatever this strange new world was, it was an escape from pressure. I no longer had to achieve because I was considered 'sick'. It became the most alluring escape. When the time arrived to plan my discharge I felt excited about having freedom, seeing friends and returning to school to finish the school year, but I was terrified of my doctor and scared of losing even a gram of weight. He was extremely strict and showed barely any compassion, and as I graduated from primary school, I didn't care to eat anything more than what was barely sustainable.

I had been awarded an academic scholarship to attend a private girls' secondary school and although I desperately wanted to start my first day there with a clean slate and no hint of an eating disorder, it became impossible to hide. My efforts to keep up the pretence of health were futile and within months I was re-admitted to hospital. In fear of being stigmatised, I was adamant that my classmates not know that I had been hospitalised for anorexia. The explanation for my disappearance became a completely physical diagnosis of 'failure to thrive'.

My second admission was to a different hospital, where I received intensive daily counselling instead of nasogastric feeding. I saw my doctor twice a week to monitor my weight and vital signs. The smallest weight loss meant an immediate re-admission to the previous hospital with nasogastric feeding and so I did everything I could to avoid this. After ten weeks of showing no visible progress other than successfully avoiding the nasogastric feeding threat, I decided to return home and to high school for the final weeks of year eight. In retrospect, returning to school was a terrible idea. While I had been in hospital, friendship groups had evolved and moved on and I was completely alone.

For the whole of year nine, I plateaued. Although I wasn't moving forwards, I didn't fall further backwards either. I met some lovely friends who, despite my timid nature and marked emotional distance, made me feel welcome. It was like I was living a double life. By school day I could blend in and almost feel normal, but from 3.30pm onwards I was an entirely different person, trapped in a separate world. During this time my parents were very loving and supportive but understandably emotionally fragile. Mum prepared my meals and we constantly argued about food. Dad took on the role of calm mediator and while he rarely showed anger, his despair was visible. While I felt ravaged by guilt for the anguish and hurt I caused, I also felt helpless and unable to eat or help myself. Mum and Dad did their very best in such a horrific situation.

By my fifteenth birthday, my lack of growth and development was a primary concern. While everyone around me continued to physically mature, my development had stopped at the age of twelve and I looked noticeably different. In school photos I didn't just look thin, I was proportionately smaller in every way, like a younger sister to my classmates. My doctor became concerned that if nothing changed quickly my growth plates would fuse and I would never go through puberty, forever remaining in the body of a child. This would not only have severe repercussions for me socially and career wise, it also meant I would be unlikely to ever menstruate and lose the option of having children.

I was still petrified of my doctor but after years of appointments and being a few years older, I knew he genuinely cared for me and wanted to not only see me well, but living a happy and fulfilling life. No matter how illogical my head-space and everyday behaviours about food were, underlying these I knew the clear reality: I was at serious risk of this illness affecting the rest of my life and it was a now-or-never situation. Unless something miraculously changed with my eating, serious medical intervention would be required. I took a leap of faith and my physical health became my top priority. Dealing with my emotions would have to come later.

Accepting tube feeding again so many years on from the first hospital experience was simultaneously both the easiest and most difficult decision to make. It was heartbreaking to find myself in the same place as four years earlier, still unable to make tangible progress or do anything to help myself, yet it was a relief to have the relentless, overwhelming pressure to keep up the fight taken out of my hands. The tube could now do all the work. I just had to be patient, let it help me, and continually remind myself that this was all for the greater good.

Halfway through year ten I left school again and started tube feeding. As it was anticipated to be a lengthy process, my parents agreed to support me in doing it from home, which seemed a much more comforting option than returning to hospital. For the next six months my parents became full-time carers, transporting me to weekly doctor, psychologist and growth specialist appointments, and making regular visits to the hospital to collect tins of tube-feeding liquid, then preparing these and administering them via the feeding machine. Although I was never afraid of becoming fat, I was absolutely terrified to think what having a healthy body would mean for me. The prospect of having a body that would grow and mature physically excited me, but I felt completely unequipped to handle the flood of expectation and need for perfectionism that becoming healthy again would bring.

During the six months at home my school was supportive from a distance, but I became progressively isolated. Some of my school friends visited every now and then, but I made little effort to keep in touch. It seemed pointless. We were living in completely different worlds. While I kept in regular email contact with a couple of friends who were travelling a similar journey to me, I was mostly isolated.

Creative pursuits became a lifeline for me during this time. I filled journals with disjointed sentences and inspirational quotes. They became a safe place to pour out the horrific emotions that I was too scared to voice. I started creating greeting cards and sold them to local newsagencies and gift shops. Incredibly, I found confidence to walk into shops with a tube dangling from my face and ask managers to sell my cards. It was challenging, but an entrepreneurial spirit emerged in me and the card orders kept me going. Some teachers and family friends also commissioned artworks. As I was physically tied to a machine for most of the day and night, these activities kept me occupied and sane.

Since my malnourishment was so profound and my body's growth receptors were in hibernation, I needed the equivalent of the nutritional requirements of two fully grown men to kick-start the growth process. The amount of concentrated liquid pumping into me made me feel constantly nauseous and physically uncomfortable. One of my biggest goals was to get my driver's licence the day I turned sixteen, so I stuck P-plates to my feeding machine. They constantly reminded of my need to see over the dashboard for driving and so the feeding liquid, literally hanging over my head, seemed much less scary.

Nearing Christmas of that year it became time to take the tube out and return to eating. After so many months of relying on the tube as a safety blanket, having it removed meant only one thing: maintaining my health, which had taken months to achieve, was now completely up to me. As I had only been eating food here and there, the level of responsibility and expectation was crippling. I had not learned anything about eating for health and growth over the past six months. For the first time in years I was tantalisingly close to a critical turning point where my body had the nutrition and physical health needed to kick-start my growth, but the minute the tube was removed, my weight started to plummet and the past six months began to slip away.

In the days following Christmas, I returned to my doctor. I had lost a significant amount of weight and we all felt defeated. We all sat in his surgery, speechless and completely still while my doctor cried. My doctor had almost become a part of our family; he rode the highs and lows with us as both a doctor and coach, and was as emotionally involved in my progress as my parents were.

My psychologist suggested I go to a clinic in Sydney and be admitted for a three-week intensive inpatient program to learn how to eat again. I resisted the idea, exhausted after months of emotional distress and lacking motivation to resume the fight, but my parents and doctor were adamant. The next day, my parents and I flew to Sydney and suddenly I was surrounded by a ward full of frail, emaciated eating disorder patients. It was confronting and scary and being in perhaps the best physical condition I had ever been, I felt completely out of place.

The program was strict, very reward and punishment driven and draconian in its approach. We were all required to eat meals and snacks together in the communal dining room. After not having eaten for so many months, I found the quantities enormous and while the others all seemed to eat their meals, for me it felt impossible. I wanted to eat because I wanted to grow, but I just couldn't physically manage the volume of food.

The nurses didn't understand my background story or realise what the previous six months had involved. As far as they were concerned I was being a non-compliant anorexic patient. I spent most of my day behind the nurses' desk being punished, when in fact the volume of food I was consuming was far beyond the quantities I had managed in years. Some nurses were verbally abusive, which shocked me.

As a quietly spoken, well-mannered girl, I suddenly found myself defensive and defiant. From my private bedroom, the view from the window showed the most spectacular view of the Sydney Harbour Bridge and skyline. I watched beautiful sunrises, sunsets and even a lightning and thunder storm. It was an ironic experience, being privy to witnessing such magnificence behind the safety of glass, but also being trapped by the glass inside a world that felt just as volatile and unpredictable.

Somehow, the negative environment began to help me. I started to protect myself from the constant criticism and punishment, becoming my own coach and motivator. I set my own eating goals and private milestones, gaining my own momentum. Although I could never reach the requirements of the program, my own personal achievements were huge. My parents were completely encouraging and proud to watch my determination for turning the horrific admission into a positive experience. After two weeks, I had managed to turn around the weight loss and taught myself how to eat enough to maintain my weight.

My lifeline throughout the longs days of being reprimanded and punished were regular visits from Dad and occasional day passes to get out of the hospital. Mum had returned home to manage the house and so Dad and I spent wonderful father–daughter afternoons together exploring Circular Quay, shopping and, for the first time in years, eating lunch, afternoon tea and dinner out in cafés and restaurants. Since my brother and sister from Dad's previous marriage both lived in Sydney, we also had some great family times.

Both Dad and I knew that while the clinic environment was horrific and toxic for me on one hand, on the other I was surging ahead and I had to last it out for only a week longer. I was discharged a day short of three weeks. I was desperate to return home in time to start year eleven and although I should probably have stayed in the clinic longer to consolidate my progress, we took a leap of faith that the past three weeks had provided the turning point I needed. For the first time in years I trusted myself and felt strong and ready to re-enter the real world and whatever pressures that came bundled with this.

The first day back at school was terrifying – I had completely lost touch with most of my friends and, after my second disappearance from school, my whole year group had cottoned on to the truth that my health problem was much more than failure to thrive. Although my body was physically healthy and I was eating well, I found myself completely drained by the end of each school day. I was not used to walking around a school yard between lessons and my brain wasn't used to so much academic stimulation.

For a while I was worried I had actually forgotten how to learn. I just couldn't seem to retain the information I was reading in text books, recall the Japanese grammar or vocabulary that had always come naturally to me, or comprehend the simplest of maths problems. My doctor reassured me this was completely normal after so many months being 'out of the game', but it frustrated me greatly and my perfectionist tendencies began to surface. Keeping up with the academic demands of senior school was even more challenging because half of my energy and time was still spent going to regular medical appointments, making myself introduce new foods and maintain a level of food intake that would allow me to grow.

A few months into year eleven, I saw my first signs of growth. My doctor measured my height and I was 0.4cm taller. It was the best moment. My doctor started grinning, which turned to laughing, and when he told me, I insisted we check three times to be sure. This tiny height change became a huge incentive to keep up everything I was doing.

Another was the school trip to Japan. This had been on the distant horizon ever since I dropped out of school for tube feeding. Getting there seemed impossible, but with the progress I had made, my doctor, psychologist and parents allowed me to go. It was such an amazing trip for the cultural and social experience as well as the unique challenge it provided with a whole new range of foreign foods, customs and etiquette. I didn't just survive the trip; I came through it with flying colours. I had experienced the world, I had handled the food and, most importantly, I had looked after myself.

I completed year eleven and was awarded academic honours. Although I still felt the desire to excel in every subject, for the first time ever I gave myself a break. I aimed for good marks, not top marks. If I was having a rough day I made sure my primary focus was to look after my health and state of mind, even if it meant I didn't complete every assessment or do the normal exam that my classmates did. I was emotionally fragile and often needed to take 'mental health days' and my school, despite having a strong academic focus and priding themselves on cultivating ambitious, brilliant students, supported me.

During that year, I came into contact with Adèle Basheer, director of the inspirational greeting card and stationery company Intrinsic Enterprises. We immediately clicked and Adèle started to mentor me with my creative work, becoming a huge source of inspiration over the course of the year. Adèle's mentoring extended far beyond just creative work. She became a powerful source I turned to for guidance, personally and emotionally, as I reintegrated myself into the world. Adèle came into my life at the perfect time and I'm certain that if I had met her any earlier, she would not have been able to help me.

By the beginning of year twelve I had noticeably grown and although I was still small – genetically, I was always going to be – when putting on my school jumper, I blended into the year group and looked just as much a final year student as the next girl. Sometime during that year I got my first period, which was another tangible sign that my body was well and functioning as it should.

Academically, year twelve was a challenge. I put a lot of pressure on myself to excel and achieve brilliant marks, yet I was also determined to achieve some sort of balance. Among the more academically involved subjects, I had the opportunity to take a subject that allowed me to pursue my entrepreneurial side and develop my greeting cards business. I designed a range of cards for the Butterfly Foundation and had a launch exhibition. Among the English essays, maths equations and psychology reports, the creative opportunities this subject allowed gave me such joy. Throughout year twelve I also made the decision to not continue with counselling. I felt strong enough take on the year solo and I just wanted to focus on getting through the school year. Most of all, I no longer wanted to have any attachments to anorexia and being sick.

I never returned to anorexia. I could never allow myself to regress into such a horrific, painful existence. I was too committed to life and to living to let that happen. My future finally looked bright and the idea of leaving school behind to travel, explore the world, study, create and meet new people was exciting beyond words. I was a young woman on a mission and I could see the bigger picture.

For years, my heart was set on studying psychology at university after I finished school. I listed it as my first preference when completing tertiary study applications and while my final result was far higher than the entrance ranking I needed to be accepted, at the last minute I switched preferences. I enrolled in visual communication at the University of South Australia, a degree that required a ranking almost half as high as psychology. I decided this was my chance to get away from my head, the complex emotions and ambiguity, and I didn't feel ready to commit to the six years of demanding academic study psychology required. It was time to live a little – to have fun, explore my creativity and taste real freedom.

It was to be one of the greatest life decisions I have ever made. My three years studying graphic design were perhaps the best years of my life so far. I met the most inspiring, creative and dynamic people and made beautiful lifelong friendships. I moved out of home in my second year to experience complete independence and freedom. Living in a share house with friends was so much fun, and I experienced many rites of passage typical for a young adult – parties, casual work and dating. Although I'm certain that pure graphic design is not what I want to do forever, for the past few years it has felt completely right.

As I graduated from university, I undertook a project to reflect upon my eating disorder, entitled 'Chrysalis: Unravelling Anorexia'. In partnership with Aceda, South Australia's peak not-for-profit organisation supporting eating disorder sufferers, I created my first commercial collection of artwork using photography layered with journal excerpts. I exhibited these as a travelling exhibition throughout metropolitan and regional South Australia. The artwork collection was published as a book. Chrysalis, the protective case under which a butterfly prepares for its first flight, became my creative approach to making peace with my eating disorder journey and coming full circle. It has been an incredible experience and allowed me to truly take flight.

I believe that having an eating disorder has almost allowed me to live a second life. If I had never travelled this journey, I may never have discovered the immense gratitude I now have for life, or developed such an insatiable drive and passion to make my life meaningful. I will never go back. I know my mind too well and could never hurt myself again or deny myself an authentic, fulfilling life. There is simply too much to explore, savour, taste, imagine, experience and love in the world.

Emma Kate's Recovery Tips

1. Using creative processes for self-expression can help you to describe the indescribable. Creativity is a powerful and soothing outlet. There is no right or wrong way to express yourself, it is the process of creating that's important, not what you end up with.

2. Consider writing a commitment to recovery statement. This was first introduced to me as an activity in group therapy. It can be a very powerful tool for articulating how you are going to commit to your health and life. I write commitment statements inside the cover page of my journal at the beginning of each year.

3. Surround yourself with beautiful colours, inspirational quotes, photos of faraway places and greeting cards on your walls, bedside lamp, bathroom mirror, fridge and diary. You deserve to be surrounded by beauty, colour and inspiration.

4. We all have days where nothing seems to go our way and I think the best thing to do at such times is to challenge yourself to write a gratitude list of things you are thankful for. If you can't write a long list, finish the sentence, 'Today I am grateful for . . .' There is always something to be grateful for.

5. Eating disorders are often steeped in beliefs of needing to be perfect. Challenge yourself to do exactly what would not be 'perfect' in any situation, to know that life goes on if something is not precise! If you feel the need to make your bed perfectly each morning, challenge yourself to leave it

unmade. Thinking of this as a personal challenge helps to break the compulsion and expectation of yourself.

The Finishing Line

George's Story

A shy boy lacking in confidence, George is now a highly motivated and successful ironman. His experiences of both anorexia and a long-term binge eating disorder were deeply intertwined in his athletic pursuits, but also his recovery, which he achieved with the help of a coach and a psychiatrist, as well as his own tenacity and will to be eating disorder free.

I grew up in a very traditional Greek household in Melbourne with my dad's Greek customs far outweighing those of my Australian-born mum. My parents ran a motel, which often meant long work hours and a great deal of time away from home, especially for Dad. Both of them were very strict. They never gave in to demands or tantrums but I believe that was a good thing, as it taught me about respect and boundaries from an early age.

I got along well with Dad in particular when I was young, but in general I have always been quiet around my parents. As a young boy, I never really understood why they had to work so much, which I believe lead me to resenting them somewhat. As a result, I never really opened up or developed as strong a connection to them as I would have liked.

Both Mum and Dad were very protective of me. I was not allowed to ride my bike on my own until I was fifteen, and if I ran an errand I had very strict time limits in which I had to be back. There was no leeway. I spent quite a lot of time in my room as a boy and always enjoyed my own company, happily playing alone. My brother is physically and mentally disabled but we played together and had a normal brotherly relationship. He had a lot of operations as a child, but I never remember him receiving any more attention than me. Everyone loved Michael and we went to the same school together, which I thought was great.

A big part of Greek culture is food and there was always plenty in our house. I ate lots growing up but I burnt it off quickly as I played a lot of sport. I ate whatever and however much I was given and there was a rule in our household that you never commented on what or how much someone ate – to do so was considered rude. Mum and Dad always appeared to me to have a positive relationship with food and I never recalled either of them being concerned about their weight or appearance.

I went to the same private co-ed school throughout primary and high school. I had nice friends and got along well with others but was always a bit shy. I was more interested in sport than academics, especially football and table tennis. Whenever I was playing sport, I felt at my most confident. I managed to make it through puberty well but one thing that was always noticeable to me was that I had quite a bit of puppy fat, even though I played sport consistently.

Often at the start of summer, I would think about wanting to be leaner and I would do sit-ups for the first days of the holidays but it would never last. Even though I never hated my body, I certainly knew I didn't feel as confident about it as I wanted to. I had mates who were state-level swimmers who I thought had amazing bodies and I also believed if I lost weight I would be more attractive to girls, who had just started to come onto my radar. There's no doubt I compared myself to other boys around me and I didn't feel I measured up well.

My self-esteem went up and down throughout my teens. At times I felt OK but at others I didn't like myself at all. From my mid teens I began to struggle to imagine my future and I had no idea what I wanted to do with my life. I began to find school rigid and controlling and it contributed to me being uncertain about what life was going to be like for me once I had to leave. Rather than being excited about leaving school and all the great things that could happen in my life, it scared me. All I knew was school and home. I don't believe the pressure I was placing on myself came from school itself; it was an internal lack of confidence, where I began to worry and become anxious about how I would cope with life after school. I would look into my future and see nothing but blackness and a blank space. It was a gnawing anxiety that was with me constantly.

By my final year, I had decided I wanted to get in to a media studies course to be a sports commentator but I didn't get the marks to get in. Although I didn't realise it at the time, I immediately slipped into a depression: sleeping long hours, eating more and exercising and playing sport less. I had very little self-confidence and no idea what to do with my life. My parents encouraged me to return to school to see the counsellor, which we were permitted to do for five years after we graduated. Dad was tired of me not doing anything and believed I was being lazy. The counsellor encouraged me to apply for other courses and eventually I started a general arts degree at university.

I enjoyed the freedom of university life much more than high school. I had been so worried about what life would be like after my formal schooling years but it ended up being great, and I got better marks than I ever had previously. Despite that, the nagging insecurities I had about my body were still with me and at the end of my first semester of study, I weighed myself and was unhappy with the number I saw. I immediately began to change what I ate and increase my exercise.

I initially tried to lose weight in a healthy way, but as I began to see results I cut down my food portions more. A few months later, I stopped eating meals until it got to the point where I was barely eating anything at all. I liked getting lighter but by now I was never happy with how I looked, which made be believe the only way to fix that was to keep going. I started to weigh myself daily and became obsessed with the numbers I was seeing.

People commented on my weight loss and told me I looked good which made me want to keep going. I've always been a numbers person, mostly, I think, because as an athlete you get used to having a results-based life. I saw the numbers come down and I liked achieving in that way. I felt like I was breaking through a number and then I would set another personal best. I genuinely didn't think I was anorexic or aiming for an unhealthily low weight. I believed I was in complete control of my body and what I was doing. But I wasn't.

I would feel bodily pain from hunger but would push through it. My parents did know I was eating very little but I managed to convince them I was fine. Even if they had thought something was wrong I don't think they would have believed something like an eating disorder was happening to their son. I didn't think I had a problem, even though I felt terrible about myself. I doubted myself all the time but I kept functioning and others around me never knew.

At twenty, I went overseas on an extended trip to Greece with my family. While I continued to eat minimal amounts, there were particular sweet things in Greece that I loved and began to eat. I started to binge and put on weight rapidly. I weighed myself and hated what I saw. I immediately cut back my food intake again but I soon returned to the sweets and a terrible cycle of starving and bingeing began.

The next few years of my life felt like a blur. I spiralled out of control between bingeing and starving to the point where I was bingeing every day. It completely took over my thoughts and feelings and I felt weak for not being able to starve myself. I had a girlfriend for two years throughout this time but I managed to keep everything hidden from her. Sometimes I felt close enough to her to want to tell, but I needed to keep my secret to myself.

I binged mostly late at night when others were asleep and I began abusing laxatives. A voice started to talk to me inside my head, telling me I was weak for not being able to starve myself and that I was not as good as other people. I was deeply sad and depressed, especially at nights, but during the day I managed to hold it together so none of my friends knew. I felt desperate inside but still either unable or unwilling to seek help.

One day I looked up an eating disorder website and did a checklist for binge eating disorder, quickly realising that was what I had. I knew deep down that something was wrong. Every now and again I thought about telling someone, but I knew once it was out, I couldn't take it back. I was also petrified someone would make me stop what I was doing and I wouldn't be able to lose weight. This was totally warped thinking, as I wasn't losing weight with all the bingeing I was doing anyway. All I lost was fluid and more rational thought, and even though I knew I needed help and had looked up that website, I had no idea how to take the next step and reach out.

The voice was now constantly berating me and I had developed obsessive compulsive traits. I would walk out and back through doors numerous times and it started to take me a long time to leave the house due to the rituals I felt I had to do. I felt compelled not to touch certain things and walk a certain way, which was debilitating to manage.

I continued to be sick after university and into my mid twenties. I had started doing triathlons, which stemmed initially from running. I loved the feeling of the finishing line and, as I started to see my results improve, I wanted to do more. How I managed to train and compete while I was so sick, I don't know, but

I was trained remotely by a coach from Queensland and did my first half-Ironman at twenty-two. I did the triathlons and Ironman competitions not to lose weight but because I loved them. Despite that, I did struggle in races with questions of whether I was worth it or good enough to finish. I would psych myself out of longer races and convince myself I wasn't worthy of finishing or doing well.

I got a new coach, Mitch, who had been a professional athlete and was now studying medicine. He was a great coach and I felt connected to him from the first time we worked together. Mitch was the first person I told about my difficulties with food and self-esteem. I felt I could trust him because he was an athlete and medical student. I had realised I was never going to get anywhere as a triathlete if I didn't fix this problem, and the competitions had become such a passion, I wanted to sort things out for myself. Mitch had already asked me if there was anything affecting my performance and I had told him there was, but I couldn't tell him what. He was OK with that and told me to tell him when I was ready.

A few weeks later we met for coffee and I told him everything I had been experiencing. I was almost in tears as I spoke about it and, listening to me, he was too. He struggled to hear the pain I had been experiencing but it was good to tell him. Mitch told me it was something I needed to get treatment for and encouraged me to do just that, but I still took a few months to follow through. He was very compassionate and supportive, but for me it was one step to tell someone but another to actually get help.

We went to Busselton in Western Australia for a race but in the two days leading up to it I had barely anything to eat. This is clearly not a good thing for anyone to do, but when you are about to do a 3.8 kilometre swim, 180 kilometre bike ride and 42.2 kilometre run, it was a stupid move. I had wanted to lose more weight and be as light as I possibly could before the start of the race with no thought to what it might do to my performance or health. I managed to have a great swim and ride, but four kilometres into the run both my mind and body gave way. I finished by walking the rest of the way, swearing I would never do an ironman again.

After the Busselton race, knowing how little I had eaten leading up to it, Mitch told me I had to get help. He gave me two weeks to do something positive towards getting well and I contacted a binge eating disorder support group. I had very little money to get professional treatment and I thought a group might be OK, but I soon came to realise I needed more intensive help. I was the only man in the group and was worried the women there would not trust me, but I was glad that wasn't the case. I didn't miss a session and I do think it was helpful in some ways, especially as I met some people I am still in touch with. I realised I wasn't the only person suffering, which made me feel less alone.

I had another bad race during my time with the group. I was very stressed in the lead up and felt completely frazzled on the day of the race. I crashed my car on the way there and hated the entire experience. Mitch spoke with a friend of his, Adam, who had been an ironman and was now a psychiatrist. He asked him to help me by bulk-billing sessions, which was the only way I was going to be able to afford to see someone. Mitch told me I had no excuse not to at least go and meet Adam, which I did. He was great right from the outset and soon I began to get things under control.

I saw Adam once, sometimes twice, a week, for nearly two years. He helped me by allowing me to have someone to open up to. I didn't feel I had any hope of getting better but Adam never let me give up, encouraging me to keep going by putting one foot in front of the other. He kept persisting with me, trying to get me to not rule out that things would get better and I should keep going rather than chase full recovery right away. He also helped me realise that food was not really my issue.

I had to learn how to build my self-confidence and how to manage my life better from day to day and week to week. I learned new ways to deal with things and be better able to cope with stresses. He helped me to manage the really little things that often got on top of me and he never made me feel self-conscious about what I was going through. I felt like I had an ally against my eating disorder and it made an amazing difference in my life.

Slowly, my eating habits changed. I began to binge less and within six months I was not bingeing at all. I continued to see Adam because even though my behaviours were now under control, I still had a lot of issues I needed to work on, including not liking myself and not having a plan for my life. I had no idea when or how I was going to move out of home and I still had difficulties handling everyday situations. It took the full two years to build up my self-esteem and confidence to a solid point. I slowly began to feel more confident about me, George, as a person.

It has now been years since I binged and I no longer see Adam. It's hard for me to believe that sometimes, as I thought I may never cut ties, but I truly no longer have the need to see him. I have a great balance with food and I'm learning to harness the power of my thinking and determination by seeing a sports psychologist as part of my ironman training. I have been going out with an amazing woman, Ailie, for two and a half years, and we live together. She is a triathlete as well and we have a lot in common. It feels great to be more independent and I feel like, for the first time in my life, I have my own space, which in turn has made me feel happier than I ever have. I'm working as a sales manager, which I really enjoy and I can see a path for some great career progression, which is important to me.

I still have moments of doubt about my body but I know my triggers now. I used to be very careful of what I was eating leading up to a race and then totally relax and eat what I wanted afterwards. I soon realised that didn't work for me and so now I just eat healthily and balanced all the time. I now perform so much better in races because I am not worrying about food or my weight.

I like myself more now and am generally just a happier and more well-rounded man. I have a passion for wanting to help others with eating disorders and would even like to work in the field professionally. I want to share my story in the hope it can help people feel less alone and encourage them to seek help early, which is something I now wish I had done. I want my story to be for everyone, not just men, as I know there are many people experiencing binge eating disorder but doing so in shame and secret. I really want to be a part of helping that change. I feel very blessed to have found both Mitch and Adam to help me beat my eating disorder. I felt like the two of them were my team and I learned to use them and not hide away, which I had previously done for so long. I now know I can stop little things becoming big problems before they happen.

Being a man never impacted on me getting help or good treatment. My desire to hide and keep my illness a secret was entirely my doing and a product of the way I felt about myself for so long. I have now met many women who have felt the same way, helping us all to learn that the best way to beat an eating disorder is to bring it out in the open and seek help.

You can't reach the finishing line and the prize of a happy and balanced life if you're not actually in the race. I eventually turned up for myself and my recovery and although it took me a long time to get there, the results now are better than any number I could ever have hoped for.

George's Recovery Tips

1. Everyone is worthy of happiness and recovery. That includes you! Don't for one moment believe that recovery is something that is meant to be for everyone else except yourself and that you have to learn to live with your eating disorder. You don't.

2. Sometimes when you are feeling very low it can be hard to believe that things will get better, but they can and do. Be hopeful and take small steps.

3. If you know in your heart that you are experiencing difficulties with food, don't get too caught up in a diagnosis and especially not the thinking that you may not be as sick as someone else. Seek help as early as you can. If you think that you might have a problem, you likely do. That is your heart and rational mind trying to tell you to get help.

4. There can be a perception that it's only if you are emaciated that you have a life-threatening illness or one that is worth seeking treatment for. All eating disorders are dangerous and require professional support.

5. Do things and think in ways that support you to like yourself as a person. Building your confidence through doing things you love will help you immeasurably and create ways for you to be able to better cope with life's bumps and turns.

The Hope Box

Nikki's Story

Nikki's story is one of hope and commitment in the face of multiple issues. Facing depression, anxiety and self-harm, as well as severe anorexia, Nikki willed herself to hang on and never give up. Nikki, a young woman of courage and conviction, has a story that serves as a reminder to anyone experiencing an eating disorder that when you commit yourself to your recovery, anything is possible.

I was born and raised in the sunny beachside suburb of Maroubra in Sydney, and grew up in a loving family with my parents and younger brother. I have always been very close to my parents and I have good early memories of holidays and family time. I was excited when it was time to start school but I definitely preferred to be with adults rather than children my own age. I would much rather go out for a coffee with my mum and her friends than have a friend over to play.

I was an anxious child and liked things to be a certain way. My anxiety increased when I started school. If things weren't the way I felt comfortable with, I would often cry. I wanted everything around me to be perfect and beautiful, no doubt because I was very creative and loved to draw and paint. I wanted things to look dazzling and lovely all the time.

I initially loved school, especially the structure and getting positive feedback from teachers. This was despite the fact I needed a tutor because I was slow to learn to read and my writing and spelling were poor. By the time I was seven I had become concerned that the school was not giving me enough work to do. I was also being bullied in an exclusionary way and I had a teacher who didn't like students using coloured pencils.

My parents were taken aback when I told them I wanted to go to a better school, but they were supportive. They found a local Anglican school that had a strong academic focus and even though I was a long way behind the other kids, I loved the new environment and teachers. I didn't make any close friends to begin with, but I loved that the school had a greater focus on the arts, and within a year my grades improved and I was no longer having learning difficulties. By the end of grade four I had some nice friends and was enjoying school.

The year I turned ten I started feeling depressed. I became a very lonely and sad little girl but I never knew why. I stopped being interested in my friends and I didn't want to have them visit. I just wanted to stay with Mum. By the following year, my last of primary school, I was still depressed and, by now, highly anxious about my end-of-school exams. I wanted to do outstandingly well and I had also started to go through puberty.

I was very self-conscious about my changing body

and had no desire to grow up. The thought of getting older frightened me and I wanted to remain a little girl and be doted on. I had never really liked my body and I thought I was fat. I had tried cutting back food to lose weight, but my efforts would only last a week and I would give up. I began to believe that all the popular girls were popular because they were thin, and that was what I wanted for myself too.

I didn't know how to cope with the emotional and mental pain I was experiencing and I fell into the trap of self-harming. It sounds so horrible to say, but I liked the feeling of the physical pain. It deflected from the confused and swirling feelings I was now experiencing every day, but didn't know what to do about. I would harm myself in places where others couldn't see, but one night Mum and Dad saw my wounds when I was coming out of the shower. They were severe and so they took me to the hospital. The way I was hurting myself left strange marks on my body and none of the staff at the hospital knew what it was. I was diagnosed with cellulitis.

I was the only one who knew it was self-inflicted. I had never heard of self-harm before or even knew it was called that. It was just something I felt compelled to do. Even though it was clearly an awful thing to do to myself, it helped me to take the focus away from the emotions I was dealing with and didn't know how to express. It was a coping mechanism, albeit a very bad one. I was trying to deflect my inner emotional pain to outer physical pain.

I was admitted and put on an intravenous drip. I was petrified the entire two and half weeks I was there that someone was going to find out I had hurt myself. I thought if anyone did find out, I would be punished severely. Everyone thought they were treating a physical illness when in fact I was mentally and emotionally unwell. I had no psychiatric assessment and no one asked me what was wrong. My parents were incredibly worried and my father, who worked in the medical sector, took a very serious approach to my hospitalisation. He got every doctor he thought could help involved in my care in a desperate attempt to solve the mystery of the marks on my body, but still no one could work out what was happening.

When I went home I immediately self-harmed again and even though I tried to hide it, my parents found the injury. Again I said I didn't know what it was. I was taken back to hospital and admitted. Copious amounts of tests were done and by now I was missing a lot of school. No one could find anything wrong with me and, after three weeks, I went home on Christmas Eve. I missed the grade six exams.

My mood lifted for a short while over the summer before I started high school. I was enrolled at a private girls' school and was excited that they had a pool and drama centre and a great focus on the arts. By now I was put in extension classes and, academically, I had improved enormously. The classes were high pressure, but I enjoyed them. I played lots of sports and music and was heavily involved in arts activities. I loved being there and it was a good year for me. I found lovely friends and I started to spend weekend time with them too. I felt like I had found my place and as a result my mood lifted and I felt better about myself.

In year eight my mood dropped again. This time I

felt there was a reason, as the girls I was friends with started dating boys, drinking and going out more. I didn't want to do the same things and it made me feel like the loser of the group. They became very image conscious as well, which I found confronting. I started self-harming again and even though she didn't know I was hurting myself, Mum took me to see a psychologist because she knew I was depressed. I didn't want to go and only went for a few sessions. I was then taken to a psychiatrist who scared me. He practiced in a very dark room and most of the time I was there I stared at the floor. I don't know how, but I managed to let slip I was self-harming and was prescribed antidepressants. My parents were told and while they were shocked initially, it motivated them to help me more.

Within days of starting the antidepressants my appetite became suppressed. I was not eating and only interested in drinking and I began to lose weight. I started not finishing my meals and arguing with Mum about food. I liked the feeling of losing weight but had no knowledge of calories or what I was really doing. I continued to go to school and do well academically, but undoubtedly I was sicker than I appeared on the surface. One day I told a friend I was fat and she replied, 'Well, you're not obese, but you're not that thin either.' I clearly remember where I was when she said that, even the exact time. It snapped something inside my head and from that moment on I became doggedly determined to be thin.

I started to hear a terrible voice inside my head that told me things like, 'You're fat. You're disgusting. You can't go swimming with your friends anymore.' I was panic-stricken and I felt terrible about myself. My body image was as negative as it could be, and by the time I was fourteen my mood was much worse and I attempted suicide. As soon as I had hurt myself I was terrified and concerned I might die. I told Mum what I had done and she drove me straight to the hospital. I was admitted to the adolescent ward for twelve days and, in that time, refused to eat. I genuinely believed my life would be better if I was thin. By day eight of refusing to eat or drink, they brought in an eating disorder doctor, who told me I had to eat or I would be tube fed. I refused and so was fed via nasogastric tube for two days. I then asked what I had to do to go home and was told I had to eat a meal. I asked Mum to bring in a meal, which I ate, and I was discharged.

I had no follow-up care and at fifteen, I was in the full grips of an eating disorder. It continued to tell me not to eat and that I was worthless. Two months after I was discharged I tried to commit suicide again. I was taken to see another psychiatrist, who I hated. I loathed my body and quickly spiralled into a cycle of depression, anorexia and hospitalisations, where I often had to be restrained and tube fed. I had numerous admissions throughout year nine for both safety – because I tried to suicide – and sometimes because my electrolytes were life-threateningly out of balance.

It was while I was in hospital that I started purging. I had never done it before but being force fed made me feel completely out of control. Whenever I was at home I still went to school because I loved it. I had become isolated from my friends and the terrible cycle of being in and out of hospital went right into year ten and I became increasingly dependent on Mum.

It was decided that hospital admissions weren't working for me and instead of staying overnight I would go to the hospital three days a week to be tube fed and then return home at night, going to school four days a week. I finally connected with a lovely psychiatrist who I had been in touch with as an inpatient. He was wonderful and I was happy to see him. He would never get angry with me and constantly told me it was my job to hold on and that he and others around me would do all the work. He gave me a lot of hope and encouraged me to keep myself safe. He was the first person to understand I really couldn't do anything beyond that with where I was, and he always told my parents I was going to be OK, which I know they drew comfort from.

Unfortunately, the day program option didn't work well either and I was booked into a specialist eating disorder clinic as an inpatient for seven weeks. When I got there, I decided I would eat my way out by acting pseudo-recovered. I just wanted to be at school, but by now I thought a change of school would help me be more motivated to be there as much as possible.

From day one I loved my new school. It was very arts focused and the faculty incredibly supportive. They knew about my eating disorder and the principal wrote me a card to welcome me and helped me set up a program where if I felt unsafe I could choose some people who would stay with me until help came. He volunteered to be one of those people and I felt so cared for. Unfortunately, though, after about four months my eating disorder became worse, and it was clear that while it had settled with the excitement of a new school, it was really always there because I had never fully dealt with it.

By now I was seventeen and back in hospital. This

time was different, though, as the principal and school chaplain came to visit me. They gave me a school scarf and a teddy bear and I felt so connected to the school community. It helped me so much and I felt embraced by the school and that they wanted to be part of me getting well. I missed a lot of year eleven and it was decided it would be best for me to do a term of year ten before progressing further. My next hospital admission was the first time I really wanted to be better.

At the private hospital, where I was to spend many months over the coming years, I was surrounded by people who wanted to get well. I also felt that instead of my treatment team fighting against me, it was me and the treatment team against the eating disorder. That shift in my thinking was enormous. I always thought it was me against them, but now I didn't want to fight with my doctors anymore. I was now completely honest with my treatment team.

Slowly, I improved and returned to school for year eleven, which turned out to be a wonderful year. I became involved in the school musical, which I loved, and sometimes the deputy principal would eat lunch with me twenty minutes before the real lunchtime so I wouldn't miss out on time with my friends. The constant support of this wonderful teacher helped me to continue to enjoy school life and school became a happy place for me where I felt safe and supported. My behaviours lessened and by following a meal plan, the eating disorder ceased to rule my life. By the time of my eighteenth birthday I was well enough to go on a holiday to Thailand with Mum, which was truly amazing and one of the best experiences of my life. I felt so free and wore my swimsuit confidently and loved swimming and eating ice-cream with no thoughts about the calories it contained or how I looked to others.

The final year of school is stressful to even the most together of students and so naturally it was an anxious time for me too. I was stressed about my impending exams and I didn't get chosen for a drama group, which shattered me. I suddenly found myself in another negative spiral and no longer wanted to socialise. I became ill again very quickly as anorexia regained control of my life. I went back to the private hospital but was non-compliant. When things weren't getting any better I went home for six weeks, where we tried Maudsley family therapy.

Trying to do the therapy with a nineteen-year-old who had been sick for so long nearly destroyed my family. My brother couldn't have friends over and it was awful for Mum and Dad, who were now petrified after all these years that they were losing their daughter. My grandma died just before my exams and Mum had to organise for me to be looked after by family friends while she arranged the funeral. When it became clear the therapy wasn't working, I went back into hospital and did the last two of my final school exams there. I was in hospital when I got my results and was proud of what I achieved. I never believed I was capable of such a mark, especially while being so sick.

I was now back to wanting to be well. I came home from hospital just before Christmas and continued to go to the hospital's day program. I was working diligently with my treatment team and found an amazing psychologist, who I still see. I was pleased with how things were going for me and I started to study nursing at university.

My moods were still very up and down, however, and just before my first nursing exams I had a manic episode and was diagnosed with bipolar disorder. I was crushed. I didn't want to deal with another diagnosis and I gave up for a while as I thought now that even if I recovered from the eating disorder it wouldn't matter, as I would always have the bipolar. The stress of university exams fuelled my eating disorder and I voluntarily admitted myself to hospital where I stayed for three months. I worked as hard as I could to get well.

The most helpful type of therapy for me has been Acceptance and Commitment Therapy (ACT), where I have learned to focus on my values and where I want to be in my life. I wanted to be a paediatric nurse and travel and do aid work. I want to acknowledge the negative thoughts I have but then turn away from them and look into my future. I now constantly ask myself if what I am doing right now is going to lead me to my goals. I ask myself if refusing to eat a certain food is going to allow me to continue nursing. It is a real motivation for me to be well so I can take care of others via my work.

Realising that my doctors and team are not out to get me, but are here to help me get well, also changed so much for me. I have learned to trust them and be one hundred per cent honest because I know they are on my side. I know I am working with a team who include me and listen to me. They help me feel more in control, rather than the eating disorder being in control of me.

I have lost a lot of friends from having an eating disorder but I have a few amazing ones who have stuck by me. They tell me they want to be with me and give me hope all the time. One of my best friends came to a session with me and, while we were there, the therapist said we should find a name for my values and who I really am. I chose the name Hope, and later my friend gave me a beautiful box that has the word 'Hope' written on it. Hope has now become such an integral part of my recovery, as I have realised that the opposite of an eating disorder is hope. I want to listen to hope and be able to identify that in my life rather than what the eating disorder wants.

People are often told to personify their eating disorders to help with separation, but they are often not to personify anything else, which I think must make some people feel like there is nothing but an eating disorder inside their head. There's not. There's hope too. I have made a hope book containing all the things I think hope would say to me. It's filled with inspirational quotes, my favourite Bible passages, beautiful pictures and messages from friends and family. I have asked friends to write a letter about hope for me and my doctor has even written in it. Another helpful thing for me has been drawing on my Christian faith. I do this by being involved in my church community where I feel very accepted and loved, but also by asking God to simply to be with me and help me not feel so alone. It helps me to realise I have many people on my side.

I unfortunately had to learn the hard way that eating disorders are a deadly illness. This past year two beautiful friends lost their battle with their eating disorders. I have learnt that I need to take recovery seriously. Every person deserves a life free from this awful illness, which claims the lives of too many souls. But that doesn't have to be your story, and it isn't going to be mine.

I now fight with the strength, courage and love of the beautiful friends who I have lost. I fight not only for them, but for me as well. I see each day as a chance to start over and never lose sight of hope, passion or my dreams. It's worth it to have the opportunity to live a full life. I continue on with the love of my friends who lost their battles, and the memories of their smiles give me the hope I need.

I'm so excited about my future and one day being completely recovered, whatever that may look and feel like for me. I now work in my dream job at a children's hospital and have the privilege of helping to make them smile despite the hardships they face. I want to share my story with people. I want people to know there is hope; that recovery is hard work but is most certainly possible and worth the fight.

Nikki's Recovery Tips

1. If you have learned to externalise and name your eating disorder voice, give some consideration to naming your real voice too. It would be easy to just call it your name but you may draw inspiration from calling it Hope, Passion, Inspiration or Love. Any word that inspires you to want to get well will be the right one for you.
2. Try not to push people who love you away. This

is what the eating disorder will want you to do, but you are loved and people will want to share their love with you. Take it from them! It will go a very long way to diffusing the power of the eating disorder.

3. Find health professionals you can trust and work with. Just because someone says they specialise in eating disorders doesn't mean they will be right for you. Keep searching until you find people you trust and connect well with. They are going to be the people you lean on in hard times so it's important you can work with them.

4. Don't ever think that you are not sick enough to get help. Your eating disorder may try to tell you this, but you are worthy of help, support and love. Reach out as far and high as you can.

5. If you think someone you love has an eating disorder, don't wait for them to come to you for help. It is OK to step in and help them get professional support – the earlier the better. They might be angry with you initially but it's more important they get the help they need to begin their recovery journey.

Arriving

Elizabeth's Story

A loving and close family was one of Elizabeth's greatest allies in her recovery from anorexia, which she experienced as a young girl in rural Tasmania and into her life as a teen and young woman. It was the realisation, though, that her mental illness was not something to be ashamed of, rather to be dealt with, that saw her finally get well.

I love the fact that I come from a very close and loving Tassie family, the eldest of three girls and a boy. I spent my early years in Hobart where Dad was a successful businessman. I got along very well with my siblings and still do to this day. My parents are lovingly married and one of the greatest sources of encouragement and strength in my life. They have always believed that family comes first and they have instilled this in me as well.

When I was five, my parents bought a farm and moved to the northeast coast of Tasmania. A loving, caring woman and talented nurse, Mum left the hospital to care for us and assist Dad on the farm, a large property that produced various crops, including potatoes, beef, lamb and wool. The farm required a lot of regeneration work to bring it to a position of financial viability and we all chipped in to help rounding up sheep, sorting cattle and working on the potato harvester. I can't really think of any time in my childhood where I wasn't happy to be part of my family. My siblings and I worked, played and laughed together, and as active, enthusiastic kids, we loved growing up on the farm.

I also liked school and was good at it. I had nice friends, though there were some dominant girls in primary school, which meant I did get taken advantage of at times. I was a little naive and always the nice girl – I hate conflict – though I was never bullied. I have always placed a lot of pressure on myself with everything I do, having an underlying desire to do everything the best I possibly can. My thinking was, 'Why bother doing something if you didn't do it to your best ability?' As a result, I achieved academically and, although not naturally an Olympic athlete, I was also good at sport. Still, I found myself constantly trying to impress others and fit in; aspects of my personality that I am certain contributed to me developing anorexia.

I wouldn't say that I was a large or skinny kid, just, well, sort of average. I began to develop earlier than many of my peers and, in year six, I was much taller than other girls in my class, and even some of the boys. I found it difficult being an early developer; puberty is a difficult time for a kid and I really just wanted to blend in and not feel like I was big and tall and a bit of a freak. I was awkward and didn't speak about how I felt with anyone. I was embarrassed and just wanted the rest of my friends to catch up. I felt more self-conscious the further I progressed through high school and soon I began to think more about my body image and how I looked. I became more aware of what I was eating and began to play more sport.

In year nine, I transferred to a private co-ed school. It was a difficult transition for me. There were distinct friendship groups and, as the new girl, I didn't really fit into any of them. I worked very hard at fitting in but felt out of place for a long time, even though to those around me I seemed to have a lot of friends. There were common themes in our conversations: boys, looks, sport, school. The group of girls I became friends with were popular. They had boyfriends, were good at sport and were pretty and slim.

I thought that if I was better at sport or perhaps a little bit skinnier then maybe things wouldn't be so hard for me and I would feel more like it had been with my old friends. I learned what calories were and started running more than I had ever done before. Being successful at sport was like a trophy at school; an automatic cool that I really wanted. I got a boyfriend at the end of year nine and was playing netball, basketball, swimming and doing athletics. Being good at them helped me to not only fit in but feel more confident as well.

By the end of the first year at my new school I finally started to feel more at home. I had things to concentrate on and targets to set my mind to. I did things well and gave my all. One of the sports I had taken a particular liking to was long-distance running; I couldn't sprint to save myself but I had the will-power to stick it out over long distances.

Long-distance running is a dangerous sport for someone who has the potential to develop an eating disorder, and for a perfectionist trying to conquer the frivolous teenage world of 'cool', it was a loaded gun.

That summer I attended a music festival with my friends and it was there that things took a turn for me. I twisted my ankle, chipping a bone in my foot. I couldn't run anymore. Suddenly I found myself with unfamiliar thoughts. I was stressed that I could no longer run – now what was I going to do? My routine was broken. I had slimmed down with the training that I had been doing for athletics, but now what? I was going to get, heaven forbid, fat. I needed to eat less. I needed to gain control.

No running, my first ever exams and the end of a hard year at a new school were stressful for me and it didn't take long for things to snowball. I found myself thinking I had to eat less, run more, study harder and socialise less. This was the beginning of a peculiar set of events for me. I was always a socialiser and liked making new friends. However, socialising and food often go hand in hand, so I stopped going to social functions. Not forever, I told myself, just until I lost a little bit of weight.

It was now summer holidays and I had been getting away with eating less because I had no structure to my days. I could skip a meal and it would go unnoticed; sneak a run and no one would know. While I had never hated myself, that feeling of self-loathing certainly galloped into my thoughts once I started to really restrict my food intake. The less I ate, the worse I felt about myself and a negative spiral began. Clearly, I was not getting the nutrition I needed, which in turn was deeply affecting my thinking.

By the start of year ten everyone had noticed my weight loss, including my family, but instead of addressing it I began to eat even less. I became obsessive about food and was taken to see a nutritionist. She diagnosed me with an eating disorder, but this only made me more determined to lose weight. I thought, 'People go to hospital for anorexia', and 'If I don't go to hospital I am a failure; I can't even lose weight as well as other people.' Somewhere in the back of my mind I knew something was wrong but my dominant thought was that there was no reason I couldn't keep going, because I surely couldn't be that sick. Just a little bit more weight, I thought. I will start to eat more tomorrow. Except tomorrow never came.

The nutritionist didn't address my real problem, which was how I felt about myself and my concern for pleasing others. She focused only on what I was doing with food and that in turn made me more obsessive about it. She set me a meal plan and I would feel as though I was successful if I could eat less than the guidelines she had set out for me. How much less could I eat? The less, the better. If I ate less than the day before I was a success and if there is one thing I loved, it was being good at something. I felt I was good at anorexia. I was *really* good.

During this difficult period, my family were always there for me, especially Mum. She was my rock. The biggest thing that I regret about my entire experience is the strain that it placed on my family. Mum was determined to find a cure and took me from one doctor to another. She tried relentlessly to offer me help – help I only pretended I wanted. In reality I was pleased that no one knew how to help me because it meant that I had complete control.

By now I was missing a lot of school. I was cold and tired all the time and didn't have the energy to laugh, let alone be social. I left school early one afternoon for a doctor's appointment and while I can barely remember leaving that day, I do remember – even in the haze of my illness – what happened next. Mum took me to a paediatrician in the city. The doctor took one look at me, put me on the scales, and told Mum I needed to be taken to the hospital immediately. We checked in to the hospital that afternoon and I didn't go home for five months.

That first night in hospital was a surreal experience. I cried and I cried and I cried until I was sure I didn't have any more tears left in me. I am not sure why I was so upset. I think part of me was devastated that I had been found out and that I was going to be made to eat. I think another part of me was feeling a sense of sheer relief; relief that someone had finally taken the reins and told me to stop. Someone had done the one thing that I couldn't bring myself to do – taken me out of the hands of the monster.

I didn't have a nasogastric tube during my admission because I agreed to eat. The doctors were so worried that I might not make it through the first few nights in hospital that I was set up in the room directly opposite the nurses' desk so I could be closely monitored. I had my heart scanned as they thought I was going to have a heart attack and my blood was taken for testing. My body was in dire straits. Five days is a long time to be in hospital, but five months is almost unfathomable. There were no specialist clinics for the treatment of eating disorders in Tassie, so I was in a public hospital that really had no idea how to treat me or my eating disorder. I was on a children's ward and, despite being unwell, I was sent my school work and kept up, getting good grades along the way.

It took a long time for me to eat my way out of hospital. It was painful emotionally, and for a long time I didn't ever think I would make it out of there. The nights are the worst in hospital; they are so lonely. With nothing to keep me company but my destructive thoughts, it was a very difficult time in my life and something that I wouldn't wish upon my worst enemy. I now understood how very sick I was, but at the time and for years after I was embarrassed about the situation I found myself in. I saw a psychiatrist on an ad hoc basis, but I never liked the counsellor assigned to me, meaning the underlying emotional and psychological reasons as to why I was unwell in the first place were never addressed. I just didn't feel like I could trust her.

My parents were amazing and my siblings were too. I still feel emotional about what my hospitalisation put them through. I felt ashamed about what had happened to me and the pain I had put everyone through. I didn't want to talk about it to anyone. Eating was extraordinarily hard and there were many tears and tantrums. At times when I was weighed and had put on weight, everyone around me would be so happy, but I was devastated despite knowing it was helping me. Any weight gain made me distraught and worried that once I started, I wouldn't be able to stop. I thought I would lose control. I had often gone so far out of my way to make others happy and this was the one thing others wanted from me but I couldn't deliver. It was an ongoing battle for me, against myself.

After such a long time in hospital I became quite institutionalised. By the time there was talk of me leaving, I was petrified to go back to the real world. I didn't know what I was going to do when I got out, but Mum, Dad and my family were very supportive, as were my friends, who had always come to see me when I was in hospital. Teachers welcomed me back to school when I finally returned in the latter part of the year. Mum was scared for a long time and would monitor my exercise. It frustrated me but she was right to look closely at me because I was still plotting how I was going to lose weight.

I continued to do well at school for the next two years and finished my final year with a good score. I had really only restored my weight, though, and still hadn't addressed the emotional reasons why I'd become sick in the first place, which in my case were stress related. I maintained an OK weight during those two years but I would never say I ate really well. My body did actually support me during this time, as if I didn't eat well or missed a major meal, I would feel physically sick and exhausted. It was a reminder to me that I needed to take care of myself.

I was happy within reason, but I wasn't the old me. I still worried constantly about my body shape and the way I looked. This feeling was heightened any time I felt under pressure or stress. On days when I felt fat, it was likely due to feeling worried about an exam or school assignment. Mum was great in helping me realise this, but no counsellor I had ever seen told me this or helped me make the connection. Mum was amazing with the research she did about eating disorders and the thinking patterns that went with them.

She searched all over the world for information that could help me and it did.

After high school, I moved to Victoria to attend university in Melbourne. I studied bio-medical science but hated it, immediately slipping back into eating disorder behaviours. Mum and Dad jumped on my case, saying they wanted me to go back into hospital, not believing I could take care of myself and begin to eat better. Although I fought with them about the idea, I really had no choice but to return to Tasmania and go back into hospital for two months. Although a shorter stay, it was a worse experience for me. I was nineteen and an adult now, feeling I should know and be better. What kind of an idiot was I to make this same mistake again? I was flat; physically and emotionally. Although I had medical support, the underlying reasons why I was unwell were still not addressed. It was simply an exercise in getting me to put on weight.

After I was released from hospital I moved back to the serenity of the farm and helped my parents build a new tourism initiative that Dad was underwriting – a world-class golf course. I enjoyed being outdoors and working and it gave me time to think. I came to the realisation that I had to address what was really happening inside my head and heart in order to get well. I didn't want to keep going around in an unhealthy cycle all the time. I also started to think about having a family, believing that was something I wanted in my future. At the same time, though, there was no doubt I had ambivalent feelings about recovering and was unsure if it was what I really wanted. This was particularly the case on days when I felt down about myself and fat.

I went to Hobart to study for a year and while I did lose weight being away from Mum and Dad, I managed to catch myself before things got too bad. I began to realise that I was placing a great deal of pressure on myself that I didn't need to. I realised that people actually liked me for – wait for it! – me, not the skinny person I thought would be more popular, more fun, smarter. I did have periods where I was stressed and exercised more and ate less, though it didn't take long for me to realise that in doing this – being fitter and thinner and working harder – I wasn't living a better life.

Spending time with my friends had always made me happier and as soon as I started to fall back into the eating disorder, socialising was one of the first things to leave my life. While uni friends were going out and having a good time, I was at home worried about what I was eating or when I was going to exercise. I felt like I was wasting my life so I decided to change courses to study business and commerce in Adelaide.

It was a much more enjoyable course for me and I graduated top of my class. It was a lot of work but I felt like I had a new and more positive focus, rather than a constant drive to be thin. I really should have been taught that in hospital. If someone had only helped me understand that I needed to find a passion or something that interested me to help take away the focus I had on myself, I'm certain I might have gotten better much sooner. In the end, though, it really was a decision that I had to make for myself. Did I want to live or just fade away?

At twenty-two, I chose to do my final course placement in London. Mum and Dad were aghast at the
thought but I was determined, believing it would be a
great thing for me to do to test myself. I was feeling
better but still felt I needed to grow up and be totally
independent. I promised I would come back if I got
unwell, but I felt it was something that I had to do. I
needed to face this beast head on instead of running
away when things got tough.

Moving overseas is stressful for anyone and I did
lose weight again. However, this time, things were different. When I started to struggle, I rang Mum and
told her. I realised that it was time to go and see
someone to talk things through. We found a hypnotherapist and neuro-linguistic practitioner (NLP) who
I genuinely feel made an enormous difference in my
recovery.

I liked him right from the start. He had a wealth
of experience in dealing with people who had issues
with perfectionism and self-doubt, and he helped me
realise that I wasn't abnormal and that everyone had
challenges in their life. I quickly learned, and came
to be at peace with, the fact that many people have
issues in life they need support with. The therapist
helped me to gain insight into my thinking patterns,
which were still very destructive, helping me understand the different parts of myself. I learned that I
had a side that was very controlling about what I
thought I should and shouldn't do, and a side that was
my freer self, which wanted me to have fun and be
happy. I came to realise the controlling side of me was
dampening me down and that I had to learn to control
the control, not let it be in charge of me.

My therapist also encouraged me to start taking a liquid dietary supplement to build my nutrition up. He was clear with me that because I was nutritionally compromised I was having difficulties with positive thinking, which was something I needed to use to turn things around for myself. Slowly, I started to go out with my friends, having more fun and stressing less. I began to think more consciously about why I felt the way I did in certain situations rather than just believing my negative thoughts should be accepted. Seeing the NLP practitioner really helped with dealing with my negative thoughts and understanding the voices arguing in my head.

I stayed in London for sixteen months and returned home happier than I had been in a long time. I no longer thought of myself as unattractive and the negative thoughts that had long plagued me started to fade. They didn't leave me completely, but I now had better control of them rather than them controlling me. I moved home and caught up with old friends and I began to do the public relations for the family golf course, which was now up and running as a business.

After working for the golf course for a few years I set up a PR agency and branched out on my own. I moved back to Melbourne and it was the first move I made away from home where I didn't lose weight. It was a significant life moment for me, making me realise I had come a long way in my recovery. I still have days and times where I feel self-conscious. I am not sure if this will be something that ever leaves me, but we all have off days. The difference now is I only have these every now and then.

I have never felt more confident and happy than I do right now. I feel great about my work and that I finally know myself. My recovery journey has felt like a long one – ten years in fact – but I feel as if I have learned a lot about myself, more perhaps than many young people my age have. I wouldn't do it all over again, but I don't regret what has happened in my life either. I no longer feel the same level of frustration or anger I once did or get upset about insignificant things – as long as I am healthy and happy things can't be that bad.

I take great care of myself now by doing yoga and running, all with the thought that exercise is to feel good, not because of any goal weight or to be thin. I know now that being extremely thin is not a life that will reward me with riches, large groups of friends or fabulous social occasions, because even if it did, I would never have the energy to enjoy them all. I now know I can't do what I want with my life if I am very thin. Even if I do manage to function on some level it's not an enjoyable existence, so it's simply not worth it.

One of the biggest things I have learned from this little bump is that it is not a shameful or embarrassing thing to have an eating disorder. It was not until I realised this and came to terms with the fact we all encounter obstacles in our lives that I really knew I couldn't go back to that life. When I was younger, I didn't realise that many people have issues and problems and that they deal with these in a variety of ways, not all of which are good.

I believe it took me longer to recover because I was embarrassed about my coping mechanism, which was to control my food intake and exercise output. I know

now that it's not that I am weird or strange. I just needed help with dealing with some skewed emotions and thinking, which in turn has helped me uncover the real Elizabeth. She took a while to arrive, but she's here and not going anywhere now.

Elizabeth's Recovery Tips

1. Don't be ashamed if you are struggling with issues related to your self-esteem, weight or eating, or if you have an eating disorder. There is nothing to hide or be embarrassed about. Doing so will only keep you entrenched in being sick.

2. Don't ever compare yourself with anyone else. We judge ourselves by others' standards so much when all we should be concerned with is the way we think about ourselves. Everyone just wants you to be you.

3. Do things that you love and make you happy. Paint, do yoga, go for walks, start a business – create and build something. When you find a passion, you think about food and your body less, which is a major step to recovery.

4. Lean all you can on people who love you and want to help, but don't rely on them solely. You have to be in the driver's seat to become well – you can't recover if you are just a passenger. You must find a strong desire to get well, knowing that life is wonderful once you recover.

5. Know that it is normal and OK to occasionally have thoughts and feelings that may not be entirely positive. We can't be up all the time and

everyone has down days. It's how you deal with those days that is the most important thing, not that they are there in the first place.

An Intuitive Heart

Laura's Story

Laura's story highlights how striving for perfection can deeply and negatively impact our self-worth and how her time working in the health and fitness industry made her eating disorder worse. Now living a life free of dangerous dieting, Laura is a champion of intuitive and mindful eating, and helps others to feel at peace with their bodies and food.

After spending the first few years of my life in Adelaide, my family moved to England. My dad's family was there and it was seen as a good move for his career. We stayed in England for five years and I had my first experience of primary school there. I never really loved school, but at the same time I didn't hate it either. We returned to Adelaide briefly and then later we moved permanently to the Central Coast of New South Wales. The transition to different schools wasn't easy. I did make friends, but it was often hard fitting in. I was blessed, however, to always feel very safe and loved at home. We have always been a family that says 'I love you' every day, which I think is great.

By the end of primary school, I felt as though I didn't really fit in well anywhere. It was almost as if I thought I wasn't good enough to be friends with certain people. These feelings were created from assumptions I had made about what others thought of me. My confidence and self-esteem were low and I didn't feel that great about myself. I just passed through school and was never really a great student except for food subjects.

I was an absolute perfectionist and if I didn't get perfect marks or do something exceptionally well, I gave up and often decided not to try. This was a pattern of thinking and behaviour that I carried right through high school and into university, but is something that I've only really become aware of in the past few years. I never really tried hard enough because I knew I was never going to be perfect. This lead to me thinking, 'Why bother?' For me it was entirely about the destination and not the journey.

When I was fifteen, I started to binge on all different types of food. I would start out trying to eat perfectly every day but it would never last. I was constantly telling myself I would start over the following day – a classic dieting and bingeing cycle. How I tried to eat at the beginning of every day was very dependent on how bad my binge was the day before: if it had been particularly bad I would barely eat all day.

My brain and body clearly couldn't cope with doing this and so I would tip into a binge. I felt an urge to eat perfectly all the time and I never felt good enough. I had quite a few friends who were naturally slim, which made me one of the heavier girls in my group. Having said that, I was very healthy, but in my head

I was much larger than them. I compared myself to them constantly and didn't like the way I measured up. My disordered eating and cycle of dieting, starving and bingeing was now entrenched and would go on for years. I kept my behaviours well hidden and would often get up in the middle of the night to binge. My parents may have noticed what was going on, such as food missing from the fridge or cupboards, but they never said anything.

I hated that I couldn't be perfect and stick to the rules I was making for myself, and I beat myself up constantly. I have a diary from this age that is riddled with food- and weight-talk and the rigid steps and rules I would make up for myself to follow. I constantly wrote that I would get through and stick to the rules the following day but I never achieved that perfection. Clearly, I was setting up expectations for myself that no one, including me, was ever going to be able to achieve.

I lost a lot of weight in my final year of high school for our end of year schoolies trip. I began to exercise a lot more and cut out more foods from my diet. I was going on the trip with the two thinnest girls in my group and I was terrified to go away with them being the size I was – or *thought* I was. I wanted to lose weight so I didn't feel as self-conscious around them. I wanted to be as skinny as I could in their presence. I was happy that I lost weight and had finally stuck to something and got results. I felt a great deal more confident about myself, and the girls I went away with commented on my new body positively. Everyone wanted to know how I did it, which spurred me on to do more, but really all it did was make the cycle I was in even more vicious.

When I finished high school, I went to university to study teaching. I really wanted to study nutrition but didn't get into the course. I wanted to learn more about food solely so I could help others lose weight like I had done. I genuinely didn't realise anything was wrong with me. I felt great about my body for the first time since I was a child and I wanted to help others have that feeling too. Clearly, I thought about weight loss in very simplistic terms and believed that being thin made you happy. Now I know better.

University felt very much like high school to me. I didn't have a lot of confidence in myself, despite my weight loss, and again I found myself wondering why I didn't seem to fit in well with the peer and friendship groups around me. I did have nice friends, but I still felt I wasn't good enough to be friends with more popular people. I managed to maintain my thinness chiefly through a great deal of exercise and disordered eating. I was constantly dieting, bingeing and starving. I tried everything to lose weight except, interestingly enough, marketed diets. I made up my own meal plans based on what I thought others were doing. I looked at the behaviours of thin people, but would never ask them what they did. I would just assume they did certain things to lose weight and then create a behaviour or pattern from that.

I felt lost. I wasn't passionate about teaching, which made me feel low, and I struggled greatly with negative body image. When I finally changed over to study nutrition I became a lot happier, as I was finally doing something I wanted to do. I was passionate about food, despite my issues with it, and wanted to learn more about it. My eating and body image improved slightly and I became more confident in myself and who I was hanging out with. My eating disorder was still very much there, but it did settle somewhat.

By the end of my nutrition degree I was in my mid twenties. I was doing a personal training certificate at the same time with the aim of being a nutritionist in a gym, still with a focus to assist others with their weight-loss goals. I had to do a placement in a gym to complete the certificate and that was where I started using my degree. I found myself thrown into an environment that was fuel for my eating disorder. I was soon to realise that in the health and fitness industry there are a lot of people struggling with the same issues, many of them extremely obsessed with food and their bodies.

The first gym I worked in was all female. Every day I helped women lose weight by showing them how to use the equipment and placing them on diets. I'm ashamed to admit it now, but I gave them very strict diets and would weigh and measure them every week. It was what was done in gyms. The diet I recommended was completely unrealistic and many clients would come back to me saying they couldn't do certain aspects of it or that they had to go to a birthday party and they had cake. I was trying to get them to eat as perfectly as they could, which I should have known from my own experiences would not work.

I was at that gym for five years and during that time I was at my thinnest and extremely underweight. A lot of people were concerned about me but I thought I was fine and still needed to lose weight. I genuinely thought I could never be anorexic because I loved food so much, but I lost my period during this time for two years and so have only recently realised that I was anorexic. I felt I was on show at the gym and that other women were looking up to me as an example of thinness and health. I also received lots of praise from others and this egged me on. They would ask me how I did it but little did they know the answer was to literally not eat.

I'm ashamed to admit that I was a nutritionist during that time. It was a very lonely and sad time for me. Presenting myself in one way at the gym and then living this secretive life obsessed with food when away from there was torturous. I became more obsessive in my behaviours and very anxious because I so desperately wanted to keep my thinness. Slowly it dawned on me that something wasn't right and I realised I was going to have to do insane things to maintain my weight. Living a double life and not being a good example also started to get to me – I became petrified that I was going to get found out.

When I was twenty-eight, I applied for another job at a gym that was being built. The owner wanted everything to be perfect and for some strange reason I was very attracted to that! I wanted to be a part of it and I became a trainer and nutritionist at the new gym where things quickly got worse for me – if it was even possible. I found myself feeling I needed to be even more perfect in this perfect environment. My bingeing became out of control; worse than it had ever been.

I would go home after work and if I hadn't done an exercise session I would binge. My perfectionism was extreme. My confidence took a massive blow because

I wasn't the 'hot trainer' that fitted into the gym the way I wanted to. I wasn't perfect and so I felt like I didn't fit in at all. Even though I didn't know it at the time, I felt so low I'm sure I had depression. I felt incredibly sad, lonely and isolated, which no one realised, and I constantly felt very ashamed. I was engaging in these terrible behaviours but was meant to be a perfect nutritionist and trainer.

The only positive thing in my life during this time was marrying my husband, who I had known since I was twenty-one. It was a lovely, wonderful relationship and the one part of my life that was working well. I was having terrible mood swings, though, and I am certain he knew something was not right with me. I wrote him a letter once to tell him I had eaten a tub of ice-cream and was upset about it. He was supportive, but because I didn't tell him the full story he could never understand how I was really feeling. I was reaching out for help but was very subtle about it.

I told my boss at the gym that I felt I had a problem, but again I was not fully honest with what was really going on. I told her I had a constant desire to lose weight and she was supportive and told me that I needed to accept myself and know that I didn't need to lose weight. She didn't want me to go on thinking the way I was, but after that one time we never spoke about it again. I finally realised that I had a problem I needed to deal with and I left my job at the gym a couple of months later.

After working for others for so long I wanted to do things my way. I didn't like the traditional fitness industry anymore and I wanted to develop a more balanced approach to health. I recognised now, though, that I needed to get help to do that. I met a psychologist via sharing an office with her at the gym and I ended up seeing her myself. Counselling helped me come to many realisations about myself and it was a great learning and growth experience.

Talking things through helped me enormously and I soon realised I had been comparing myself with others to the point where it was literally making me sick. I learned that I had been placing incredibly unrealistic expectations on myself and that trying to be perfect had got me absolutely nowhere. I had been so hard on myself for so long. The psychologist constantly held me accountable for my actions. It wasn't a straight road to recovery and I had many ups and downs, but she challenged me on each aspect of the disorder, which helped me to break it down piece by piece. She constantly held me accountable for my thoughts and actions. Slowly, my behaviours diminished and I became more balanced.

I also learned about intuitive eating through my own internet research and I immediately felt connected to it. I felt like I had finally found something that resonated with me. I started to listen to my body and heart more and learned to eat mindfully and appreciate food. When you're dieting it's all about calories and portion control, but intuitive eating is all about eating food not because it is healthy or not because you 'should' eat it, but simply because you want to eat it and it feels right. It's also about taking your time to enjoy food and not see it as something torturous and controlling.

I had never eaten like this before; I had always eaten for weight loss, never enjoyment. I learned to eat to feel good and I would ask myself quite a lot, 'Is eating this going to make me feel good?' If not, I wouldn't eat it. Eating this way dramatically reduced the dieting, bingeing, starving cycle I had been engaged in for so long. Every principle of this way of eating made sense to me. I was so sick of starving and bingeing. I wanted to feel good for once. It also wasn't another diet or fad. It was something I could see myself doing for the rest of my life.

Once I wasn't constantly trying to lose weight and be someone I wasn't, I relaxed a great deal. I just got on with my life and started really living for the first time. I felt a sense of freedom and happiness I never had before, which was wonderful. When I think back to the time I had an eating disorder, I realise I never did things one hundred per cent. There was always a cloud hanging over my head of being worried about what I looked like. I remember walking up on stage to collect my degree at graduation, frantically wishing I'd lost weight for the occasion. I had worked so hard to get that degree and all I could think about was my weight. It clouded every moment of my life with negative thinking and unhappiness. To be free of that now is truly amazing.

I now have my own fitness and nutrition business helping others in the way they should be helped – not with diets and punishing exercise routines, but with balance and wellness. I look at my own health and that of others with a total lack of weight-loss focus now. I encourage people to eat what makes them feel good and move in the same way too, helping people to set up their lifestyle to support those things. It's really the opposite of what I have seen take place in gyms. I focus on actions and small steps people can take every day to feel good. I can't ever imagine going back to a gym – unless it was my own and I got to do things my way!

I have huge issues with the diet and weight-loss industry now. I see the damage it does in my own practice and have worked with many young women who come to see me, afraid to eat after being on the latest fad diet. They deny themselves certain food groups and are obsessed with losing weight. It's so damaging to their confidence and self-esteem, not to mention their bodies. They hate themselves but are in fact beautiful girls.

The message that the diet industry sells us all is that we need to be someone different from who we really are. We don't. We are being sold a message that we need to be someone we are not, when in fact we should just be encouraged to be who we are and love ourselves as we are. Once we know how to do that, we are so much more likely to treat ourselves better for life – and that includes how we nourish our bodies and move them positively.

Learning to accept myself and eat in a way that is intuitive and mindful was a profound help in my recovery. By learning to love and accept myself, I found I no longer wanted to treat myself so badly. I wanted to do the opposite. It terrifies me to think that I had done so much damage to my body that I was told I may never have children. I have a beautiful baby girl now, which is such a blessing, but if given the chance I would go back and tell my fifteen-year-old self to love and treat her body with a great deal more kindness and respect. I can't turn back the clock, of course, but I can believe those things about myself now. And I do.

Laura's Recovery Tips

1. Do things that make you feel good about yourself – and only those things. If you are caught in a trap of doing things that you know don't feel good, the sooner you can stop doing them, the better.

2. Don't deprive yourself of or restrict things in any way. By denying yourself food, or fun, or love, you set yourself up to have an overwhelming drive or need for those things, which can cause intense emotional pain and bingeing.

3. If you are struggling with a bingeing and starving cycle, it's important to not diet or do things like count calories. Try to ask yourself, 'What foods are going to keep me nourished and happy?' You deserve to have a balanced and whole relationship with food, exercise and your body and this is a great step to achieving that.

4. There's no such thing as a perfect person or indeed a perfect anything. Life's filled with wonderful discoveries and meaningful events but you will miss them if you're striving to be something or someone who doesn't even exist. You don't need to be perfect, you just need to be you, and that you is unique and beautiful, inside and out.

5. Reclaim your power and control. Following a commercial diet program is handing over control to a diet company. You are allowing them to dictate your food choices. Become the expert of what your body needs and what nourishes you by listening to your body.

My Today

Sophie's Story

Starting a restrictive diet after years of lacking in body confidence saw Sophie develop an eating disorder that was with her, in one form or another, from her teens until adulthood. Learning to turn away from the eating disorder, with the help of a loving marriage and the experience of motherhood, has helped Sophie realise that her life is not, and was never supposed to be, defined by a mental illness.

It has taken me a long time to realise that I am not my sad story. For many years I believed the only interesting things about me were the minor tragedies of my life – that I was given up for adoption, that I struggled to feel secure, and that I suffered from an eating disorder. Even though there were times when I wanted to just be me, it wasn't until I diligently turned my back on the eating disorder that I could even begin to create a new story. Now I am living my new story – a life that is much more fulfilling and interesting than an eating disorder could ever be.

I was adopted at birth and grew up in a humble suburb in Melbourne with my two younger brothers, the middle brother also adopted and who had an intellectual disability, and the youngest brother born to my parents. We were a Christian family so I had a happy but sheltered existence between home, a local Christian school and church. School bored me from a very young age. I found the environment stifling and, as someone who loved to be creative and think outside the square, I hated being trapped behind a desk all day. It made me dislike the classroom environment and school in general. I found I had little emotional connection to most of the work even though my grades were good.

I started doing gymnastics at ten and I quickly became aware that I was not one of the smallest or thinnest girls there. I also went away on a camp at this age and noticed one of the very pretty girls got more attention from the camp counsellors. I was not an unattractive girl, but quite mousy and plain. Those experiences planted the thought in my mind that being thin and pretty was the way you got ahead. I remember thinking, 'So that's how it works.' Pretty girls were popular. Pretty girls got attention from boys. I was not pretty, but funny and smart.

I wasn't great at gymnastics but I enjoyed it and did it for a few years. As I got older and my body changed, though, I became embarrassed at being so on display. I had always worn a T-shirt when doing gym and was very aware I didn't have the typical tiny gymnast shape. The rewards from gymnastics stopped coming as I got older and when puberty struck I didn't want to do it anymore.

Going through puberty I struggled to acknowledge that I was changing and becoming a woman. I hated having to tell Mum I needed a bra and I gave her very strict guidelines about the sort of one I wanted. I also hated getting my period and talking to her about that. She was very maternal but I did feel somewhat separate from her and even at a young age I put this down to being adopted, although I wonder now whether it was just my personality. I appreciate her now as an adult so much more than I did when younger. I think about going through puberty now and realise she was much more comfortable about it than me.

High school for me was defined by the social structure I found myself surrounded by. My friend Rebecca and I were a strong duo in a very bitchy class. We were surrounded by a lot of queen bees who were very pretty, witty and street smart. That was so not me due to my low confidence and, possibly, my personality. I never wanted to be like them but I also didn't want to be overwhelmed by them. I just wanted to be popular and liked by boys, who I was now very aware of.

I was a competitive student in high school, always striving for A+ so the teachers would be impressed. I did particularly well at subjects like English and literature, where I could inject some of my creativity. Things went along well at school until I was bullied in years nine and ten. I began to be friendly with some boys for which I was labelled a social climber. Now in my mid teens, I had started to groom myself better as well, which seemed to rile girls around me. My classmates began to talk about me behind my back and excluded me. I shouldn't have cared and it shouldn't have mattered to me, but it did. The girls stole my diary and wrote mean comments in it. I felt there was no way I could tell a teacher or my parents. The experience made me think I needed to be beyond reproach. I felt I needed to be pristine and exemplary so no one would attack me. I eventually started to cope better with the bitchy girls as I got older, but they also backed off from me somewhat, due to their own infighting.

At the end of year ten I went on a holiday to Noosa in Queensland with family friends. It was their suggestion to my parents to take me – as either respite for me or my parents – and while I wasn't really a fan of new things or environments, I went. Everyone in Noosa seemed to me so rich, glamorous and beautiful. I was from a very average-income home and family and it felt like a whole new world. I was out of my comfort zone and, without giving it much thought, I cut back on what I was eating dramatically. Everyone was so svelte in Noosa and clearly my severe dieting was a subconscious attempt to try to fit in and feel better about myself. I also got a tan and dyed my hair blonde. I made some friends who were non-Christians and got drunk and kissed a boy for the first time. In many ways it was my coming-of-age experience, but one that, with my new relationship with food, was to change the course of my life significantly.

I lost a considerable amount of weight very quickly and as I wasn't large to begin with, it was noticeable. When I returned to start school for the year, boys noticed me for the first time. I was thrilled. I was finally worthy of attention. Mum took me to see a psychologist, thinking I had a problem with food that stemmed from me being a fussy eater as a child. But the issue I was grappling with was not food. The issue was that I wanted to be thin, which I genuinely believed would make my life easier and better.

I believed being thin would help me be more popular, liked and accepted – and my experience post Noosa proved me right. The psychologist was an eating disorder specialist and while I quite enjoyed talking about myself and my life, I knew she couldn't help me unless I wanted to change – and I didn't. I was honest talking about everything else in my life, but in my heart I always knew, despite seeing her for many years, that we were never really making headway with the eating disorder and my feelings about that.

I stayed under a healthy weight for about six months until not long after my sixteenth birthday. I ate a lot of food at my birthday party and it was like a dam broke. I began binge eating and put on all the weight I had lost – and then some more – in a short space of time. My brain and body could no longer cope with the dieting and starvation. I was physically and mentally exhausted.

I spent the next two years feeling I was far too heavy for my usually small frame, and feeling more uncomfortable with myself than I ever had before. I was miles off being happy and I have diary entries from the time that I find so sad. There were times when I wanted to rip the fat right out from under my skin. I felt disgusting and despicable and berated myself every day. Somehow, I did well in my last year of school, but how I managed it I am not sure. I ended up getting an exceptional mark despite the fact I was clearly unwell.

After school I studied journalism at university, but my confidence in myself was virtually nil and I became terrified to even turn up to lectures, and failed a subject in my first semester. It was a huge shock to me as a high achiever and I didn't cope well. By now I had been on a dieting and bingeing cycle for years. I fell into a relationship and got engaged, which was supported by my family and his. We knew one another from church and school but it didn't take me long to realise I had only gotten engaged because he had asked me. After I broke off the engagement, I quickly entered another relationship and my thinking about food and myself changed again. When we broke up I poured all my feelings of rejection into dieting so I could show him how pained and hurt I was about it. It wasn't long before I was on the starvation path again. But now, aged twenty, I was good at it. I lost a lot of weight and was thinner than ever before, losing my periods and diving back into anorexia.

Mum took me to a doctor and both my parents were now asking me what was wrong. They started to weigh me every day but I found ways to deceive them. I started to take laxatives and would go from pharmacy to pharmacy to get them. I developed severe anxiety about being caught. Eventually word got out about what I was doing and the pharmacists would refuse to sell them to me. Dad went through my room and found the laxatives and made me promise to stop. But by now I was psychologically addicted, despite feeling physically ill all the time. I genuinely believed if I stopped using the laxatives I would put on weight. It was a hellish and nightmarish time; one I will never repeat again.

One night, seemingly out of nowhere, I had a panic attack. I thought I was having a heart attack. To my relief, I didn't die, but the experience shocked me. I went to the doctor the next day to get help and admitted I had an eating disorder, as well as anxiety and depression. I was so starved of nutrients I had little ability to think properly or positively and felt I had gone mad.

I had been seeing someone for a while during this time but kept everything from him. I knew I had to ring and tell him. Fortunately, I think it suited him to take care of me for a while. Over the next year I took antidepressants, which I think did help to restore healthy thought patterns, but the relationship ended. I continued studying and slowly put on weight and became better. I still felt very unsure about myself, though, and saw a Christian psychologist, who chiefly explored my spiritual side. It was helpful, but at the same time, I felt that it didn't get to the heart of the eating disorder and why I was gripped in that.

I finished university at twenty-three and started to do better. I got a job with a charity as a personal assistant and I met someone at work who I went out with for a year. During that year I went overseas on a work trip, which pushed me out of my comfort zone and I lost weight again. There was now certainly a pattern whereby every time I felt out of control I lost weight. I was only gone a couple of weeks but it had a big impact on me. My boyfriend proposed to me on my return and, vulnerable at the time, I said yes. Even though I cared about him, I think I always knew it wasn't right to get married. Still, I felt like I couldn't break off another engagement and convinced myself and my family I had to go through with the wedding.

The marriage lasted two years. He was a good spouse but for a long time I had to work up the courage to leave what I knew was not a positive situation for me. I was a comfortable weight during this time and looked after myself quite well, but I wasn't fully happy. I felt my life was lacking in creativity. There was no way the marriage would have lasted long term – I wasn't being all of myself with him so we were better apart.

After the marriage break-up I lost my appetite for about a week, which I consider to be very significant because that had never happened before. I had always had an appetite for food, even if I was denying myself from having it. I started experiencing anxiety again and lost weight. It triggered in me a desire to stay under a healthy weight because I realised it made me look sick, which in turn seemed to make me more endearing to people. I felt guilty about the break-up of my marriage and I wanted people to know I wasn't OK and was suffering. I started a new job with another charity and I slowly pieced things back together for myself. Starting work in a new place was a chance for me to rebuild and surround myself with new people. I put myself on an internet dating site but incredibly enough, the first person I met had anorexia. We went out for a few months but I kept breaking things off knowing that I didn't want to be with him long term and it wouldn't be healthy for either of us to stay together. I eventually cut ties with him altogether.

I was single for a number of months, at a low weight, but eating better. I had an ordered and structured life and I certainly would never have stepped out of the rules I made for myself around food. Then I met Callum, who was unlike anyone I had met before. He had a completely different relationship with food than anyone I had ever known. He has a poor sense of smell and almost no interest in food at all – it's just something to fuel his body with. We were engaged after a few months and then married a few months after that. Callum came to me at the exact time that was right for me and he was everything I wanted in a partner. I've felt amazing about the choice we made to be together every day since.

Reprioritisation has been the thing that has been the major catalyst for me to becoming well. For so long, my priority was my body and myself. I turned inwards in an attempt to be what I thought I should be to be happy and liked by others. Before meeting Callum, I had slowly begun to draw worth from other things around me, including starting my own business as a writer. It helped me grow in confidence and feel more able to do other things.

The charity I worked for also opened my eyes to the lives, beliefs and struggles of others. It wasn't scary to me, as it may have been in the past. It made me curious about more things. I also learned that being kind to others most often meant that kindness came back to you. I became more interested in other people and in engaging with them in a more open and sophisticated way. I became less interested in me and more interested in others, which opened up lots of new experiences and people to me. The need I had to be special, and even noticed, fell away.

Callum and I had some pre-marital counselling with a really creative and unorthodox marriage counsellor, which I loved, but a strange thing happened while we were seeing her. She advised us not to get married, believing I had too many issues to deal with. After years of telling my 'sob story' I could see how she may have thought that, but I knew it was not the case at all. I suddenly realised I wasn't my sad story or the anorexia I had experienced. I didn't want pity anymore. I wanted respect. I appreciated that I needed to tell my full story to promote more healing and, in doing so, I realised that I didn't want to hold on to it any longer. It was time to move on. I finally understood that I could choose who I wanted to be and I didn't need the illness to define me or make me special. I acknowledged – and still do, of course – that it existed, but I no longer felt I had to cling to it, believing it was the only thing I could do well.

When I fell pregnant, I felt very sick throughout the pregnancy. It changed my relationship with food once and for all. I started to see food as a fuel that I needed for myself and my baby, but unfortunately I found myself in the ironic situation of feeling and being sick every time I ate. I had spent so much of my life wanting to purge food and now I just wanted to be able to eat and have my body accept the food peacefully. I felt this way for four months, which was very difficult to manage, but I pushed through.

By the time I was pregnant with my second child, I felt quite different about my body. There's no doubt that carrying a child and having your body become softer and rounder for such a wonderful reason is very healing, but the most important thing that both pregnancies have changed for me is how I relate to food. Food has stopped being a fixation for me and has become something I see as sustenance. It has become a path to being nutritionally sound – not just for me, but my babies as well. I feel like I am eating for someone else but at the same time doing something good for me too.

So many times prior to being pregnant I had felt food was quite poisonous, but now I eat it willingly. I now also enjoy cooking, which I had never been averse to but when you are denying yourself so many foods it's not the fun and joyous experience it can be. I enjoy cooking for Callum and I'm still uncovering many foods and recipes that taste great, made up of foods I denied myself for so long. I am currently writing a book, which I am loving doing. I feel creatively fulfilled in my life, which is very important, especially as Callum, who is a poet, leads such a creative life himself.

Investing in things other than the eating disorder has been pivotal in my recovery. When I was trapped in the eating disorder I wasn't living at all and sometimes when I look back, I feel grief for the time I have lost being beholden to it. I can only look forward now, but I have lost so much time not fully being myself. Becoming involved with other people and life at a deeper level has been so rewarding. I thought I could perfect myself and people would love me, but of course that was never going to happen. I thought I'd seen it in the lives of popular girls in high school, and in the media. But attention isn't affection. If anything, being anorexic made people mistrust me. And as it turns out people love me for me.

I wish I'd been able to believe I could find happiness outside the eating disorder much sooner than I did. I could never have imagined that people could feel attractive at any other size than very thin, but you can, of course, and millions of people do. Your happiness is not defined by what you weigh – and beauty is a confidence that shines from within. I absolutely understand what it is to be anorexic and have someone tell you that you can be happier at a higher weight and not believe them. But they're right – you can be, and it feels so much better than I ever thought it could.

Sophie's Recovery Tips

1. Harnessing your creative powers can be incredibly powerful and vital to your recovery. Even when you feel terrible, you can still have a desire to write or draw or paint, and I think it's important to listen to that.

2. I think it very likely that I was not able to engage well with counsellors because my nutrition and therefore cognition was so poor. Doing everything you possibly can to nutritionally restore your mind and body is a key part of recovery.

3. Get a hobby! For a long time I made my body my hobby, which was a very negative and insular pursuit. But when you focus on other people or activities you realise how small and insignificant weight really is.

4. Find ways to become involved and interested in others. While I know it can be hard if you are feeling anxious or down, reach out to friends and

others for help in guiding you towards opportunities in which you can spend time with people where you and the eating disorder are not the centre of discussion.

5. Think of food as fuel, not as the subject of a love/hate relationship. Put it in perspective and invest in your life, not your sickness.

Tissue in the Wind

Ally's Story

Ally's story is a tour de force of heartbreak, loss and tragedy, as well as resilience, love and triumph. Her journey from a life-threatening case of anorexia and traumatic hospital admissions, to self-love and personal awareness sees her now enjoying a career as one of Australia's most talented comedic and dramatic actresses.

When you lose your parents at a young age you have to rely on a reserve of love that comes from no one but yourself. It's freeing and empowering, but very hard. Losing both of my parents before I was eighteen was heartbreaking. Growing up in Wagga Wagga as part of a country community, I often felt our family was under scrutiny and being watched. Considering what was happening with us, we were.

As an alcoholic, Mum had little ability to look after me, my sister Phoebe and my brother Doug; it was a struggle for her to look after herself. I felt much closer to Dad, even after he was diagnosed with schizophrenia when I was four. I didn't blame him for his illness but I did blame Mum – I felt her illness was a choice and self-inflicted, but of course I now know that alcoholism is a sickness too. As a child, it was the only way I could interpret what was going on with them. Mum did not cope well with Dad's illness and was unable to offer him any tangible support. He tried to commit suicide a dozen times before eventually going to live with his parents, where he received more support.

Whenever Dad hurt himself, Phoebe, Doug and I were shunted to friends' houses, where I always felt out of place, shy and uncomfortable. I often distanced myself from the negative things happening around me, taking on the role of a watcher. I disassociated a great deal, and while I often knew I was present in certain situations, I also disconnected from what was happening and didn't want to be a part of things. In my final year of primary school Mum and Dad eventually divorced. By this time, Mum had a boyfriend who she spent a great deal of time with at the pub. I spent a lot of time at my cousins' house where I was usually offered dinner, but would only occasionally accept. I felt like they were just pretending to be nice to me when in fact they were extending me love and care. Still, I genuinely felt I didn't deserve to eat their food.

I was a shy at school and painfully aware that my family was not like others. I preferred art-based pursuits like drawing, music and sewing to things like maths and history, however, my first year of high school was a positive one and I found myself in a popular group. I loved that first year and felt like I was just starting to come into my own when, for me, the worst of tragedies struck.

Three days after Christmas that year, Dad committed suicide. I was the last person to talk to him on the phone but he gave no indication anything was wrong. I immediately felt, after hearing the news, that I was not a part of the whole thing, rather that it was just happening around me. I didn't feel justified in being upset because everyone around me was so much more so. I didn't want to cry and make a fuss because I didn't feel that I deserved to grieve. I placed myself in a bubble and tried hard to protect myself as a way of coping. I couldn't feel anything apart from a lot of pain and confusion.

By the time summer was over and I started year eight, I was desperately sad and lonely. At school, Dad's suicide was on everyone's lips. I felt like they were all looking at me and feeling sorry for me, which I hated. I saw the school counsellor once but hid the turmoil I was feeling. I definitely wasn't going to talk to an adult I barely knew, and so I decided to just get on with life, even though I often cried at school from missing Dad so much. One girlfriend was amazing to me. She would talk to me as before, and offer me hugs, just being an amazing friend. It was moments and relationships like that one that made me feel a little worthwhile and hopeful.

I was emotionally raw for a long time. Phoebe didn't cope well and started to dabble in drugs. I was devastated because I loved and looked up to her so much. Teachers at school would often ask me where she was and why she wasn't at school. If I cried at school, teachers assumed it was about Phoebe, but mostly it was about Dad and the great loss I felt without him around. It served as a validation to the unworthiness dwelling within me; that I didn't deserve help, and that my feelings were unimportant. This in turn made it impossible for me to recognise my own self destruction. I was floating about, alone, like a tissue in the wind, not knowing who to turn to or who I was, nor that there was something really wrong inside me waiting to erupt.

When I was fourteen, Phoebe moved to Sydney to pursue a singing career. On a visit home with a girlfriend, I caught her friend making herself sick in the bathroom. I had no idea what she was doing and she casually told me by doing it 'you could eat anything and not get fat'. I gave it a shot and while at first I couldn't do it, after a week or so I had an outlet for my lonely and dark feelings. The physicality of purging went hand in hand with the deep black hole I had inside me. I longed to feel empty and this gave me a way.

I lost weight from my already small frame but then decided I didn't want to keep doing such a thing to myself. I stopped purging, deciding instead to simply eat foods with no fat in them. Mum was always on a diet and I had instant access to her magazines and books, which told me the nutritional content of everything and I looked for foods that met my no-fat criteria. This limited me to barely anything, but I committed and went for it on my new 'health' diet.

I had no idea I had become obsessed with the way I was eating and became very sick and very skinny, very quickly. I didn't really know what anorexia was and I also didn't believe I was important enough to have that sort of an illness anyway. I thought anorexia was for special, beautiful people in magazines. I started to read Mum's magazines and take them as gospel. I became obsessed with looking up diets and weighing food because that's what they told you to do. I also read a story about a famous Australian actress and model who had anorexia. It mentioned her weight when she was at her sickest, but I thought she was beautiful and successful. I was now fifteen years old and found myself in a place where I couldn't eat.

Mum was going through her own dramas so when she noticed what was happening with me it was just another point of argument. She could never really do anything about what was happening to me anyway and I think she just resigned herself to the fact that this was who I'd become. School certainly noticed, though, and teachers became concerned. I would ride my bike to school to keep my exercise up, but had no energy and would fall asleep in class. I couldn't eat in front of others, even if I was hungry.

My friends told my physical education teacher I wasn't eating and she started to watch what I was doing, but failed to ask me if anything was wrong. I tried really hard to eat an apple in front of my friends once, to try to fit in and be normal at lunch time, but I physically couldn't. I got really upset with myself and hid in the bathrooms and cried. I had lost all control and eating was no longer a choice for me. My weight had dropped drastically but I was too scared to ask for help and I didn't feel like I deserved the attention.

On Mother's Day when I was fifteen, I took Mum breakfast in bed. We were getting along quite well at the time and she asked me to sit with her, suggesting I have some of the pancakes I had made. I refused and said, 'I can't.' Mum said the best present I could give her if I couldn't eat the pancakes would be to have a check-up. I reluctantly agreed and we went to the hospital because it was a Sunday.

The doctor who saw me said my heart was in danger of stopping. He was very unhappy that I had been sick for so long with no medical attention. I was told I could be voluntarily admitted or I'd be placed in a psychiatric ward against my will. I didn't want to go into the psych ward because I didn't think I was mentally ill. I was also petrified of the stigma because Dad had been mentally ill and I didn't want to end up like that. I felt normal, but misunderstood. It was like I was a wrongly accused criminal, being one hundred per cent sure I was innocent but about to be locked away like I was guilty. I didn't want to be hospitalised but chose to go in voluntarily. I was placed on a children's ward for a week and got sicker. I was so upset about being there and was angry at everyone around me. I was in my own room and very isolated.

I received no counselling. I just had food placed in front of me and was told to eat. They quickly realised I wasn't getting well and I was sent to a children's hospital in Melbourne for re-feeding. I was sent on my own in an air ambulance, which was terrifying. The idea was to get my weight up so I could go to a clinic for treatment, but my family was never going to be able to afford it anyway. I was at the mercy of the public health system and it didn't treat me well.

I simply couldn't eat in the hospital, even if I'd wanted to, so I was threatened by the nursing staff with a nasogastric tube. To avoid the tube, I ate small amounts and a nurse would sit with me and watch me eat. I was OK with that as I had never really had food cooked and brought to me before. Mum wasn't much of a cook and we'd never sat down for a meal as a family. It was an eat whenever you were hungry sort of situation, with not a great deal of nutritious food.

I was on a protocol, which meant I was not allowed any visitors, except Mum and only for half an hour a day. She came to Melbourne and stayed in nearby accommodation for two months and in that time we became closer. The fact she was so restricted in seeing me made me feel like such a bad child and that I wasn't worth spending time with. The treatment and restriction of love and affection, which I needed so badly, was the worst possible thing for me at the time. It was horrendous and I certainly know now that being treated in such a punitive way does not help people get well. It makes them sicker. I constantly felt like a troublemaker. There was no compassion and no encouragement. I didn't understand what was happening to me. I still didn't even think I was sick! It was as if I was waiting for them to kick me out for pretending.

I eventually broke down crying in front of the nursing staff and said I couldn't eat any more. They sedated me and put a tube in while I was unconscious. I woke up with it in place and felt totally violated. I pulled it out and they put it straight back in. I had lost control over my own life. Looking back, I see that I needed someone to talk to, someone who would ask me why I couldn't eat, but no one did. The hospital sent me home to the Wagga hospital with the intention to transfer me to a specialist eating disorder ward in a Sydney hospital.

I had been in hospital for two months and had not walked at all during that time due to the strict protocol placed on eating disorder patients. I had bed sores and barely any strength to stand on my own. The first night in the Wagga hospital I decided I couldn't stay in hospital one minute longer so I put on my hoodie and, like a James Bond spy, walked out the hospital. No one saw me or tried to stop me. I was shaking all over and ran through the emergency department into the night. As I ran to the 7–11, I tore out my nose tube and rang Phoebe's boyfriend, Paul, to come to get me. He and Phoebe were about to have a baby, which was the one thing I was excited about in my life. She was in a better place and I thought she and Paul would listen and understand.

Paul picked me up and we drove around in the dark for hours. He told me I was creative and his favourite artist and that I had to try harder to get well. Talking about things and hearing his encouraging words helped me and began to change my thinking. He took me back to their home and by then Mum was there. They told me they had to take me back to the hospital but I flat out refused. They said I had to do something to prove I was serious about my recovery and so I said I would have a cup of tea with full-cream milk and sugar. I drank it and from that moment on something in me shifted.

I wanted to be free. I began to talk about things and tried to eat more and concentrate harder on getting well. It was an improvement, but I was still only eating what, to me, were very safe foods and despite being sick for so long, I still had not gotten any significant help. I was soon well enough to return to school and when my nephew was born I began to spend more time with Phoebe and Paul. The little guy was so healing to me and in many ways it felt like as he was learning to live, so was I.

I finished my final year of school and moved in with two girlfriends. I worked a few small jobs in cafes and retail shops and slowly I felt like things were beginning to fall into place. Just when I started to feel more secure, Mum was diagnosed with a brain tumour and from the day she found out, it was only a few weeks before she died. I was heartbroken; especially as in the months prior to her death she had stopped drinking and started to develop some nice friends through a local church. I was so sad to think how great her life might have been if she hadn't got sick. It finally seemed like she and the rest of my family were on a positive path.

I remember being at Mum's funeral and feeling people look at Phoebe, Doug and I and shake their heads, wondering how we would cope. I certainly had the feeling that a lot of people expected me to relapse massively, and as easy as it would have been to give up right then and there, I gained strength from the one thing that Mum had always given us even among our chaotic life: unconditional love.

I had to be strong, for my sister, my brother, my nephew – and for me. I was still very underweight and now both my parents were gone. Phoebe had a new partner, Steve, who had been a friend of hers for a long time. He had promised Mum he would look after us before she died and he did. Phoebe, Steve and I spent a lot of time together with my nephew and as I slowly continued to get better, I began to think more about what I wanted to do with my life. I'd always been artistic and so I put myself through university, studying graphic design. It was a great healing time. I made wonderful friends and really blossomed. By the end of my course, my love for design and art was strong but I realised I was much better at talking about and presenting my projects than doing them.

After university I was ready to move away from Wagga and so went to Melbourne. I found a job in graphic design, but when I broke my elbow the enforced time off was the perfect opportunity for me to start thinking about how I could use my newfound love of talking and presenting. Secretly I had always dreamed of hosting a children's TV show. I thought, 'Why not?' and enrolled in a presenting course, at the end of which I was given a show reel. I sent my reel out and volunteered at Channel 31, hosting and working behind the scenes at a music show called *Noise TV*.

I found myself incredibly into presenting and interviewing, and the crew I worked with were so encouraging and positive. I began to fully focus my thoughts on developing a TV career. Thinking back to those terrible months when I was in hospital, I concentrated on what I really wanted for myself and why, and I'm certain that positive thinking started to make amazing things unfold for me.

An opportunity presented itself to be the host of the 3 Mobile cricket show. Before long, I was travelling Australia interviewing Adam Gilchrist, Brett Lee and Ricky Ponting. This opened me up to further opportunities and gave me amazing footage for my show reel. Through Phoebe I heard about another show that was looking for a host. The show was *CyberShack* on

Channel Nine and was about video games and gadgets. I thought it would be right up my alley with my graphic design know-how and, lucky for me, so did they. I had been setting intentions so powerfully and positively and finally someone believed me. The producers loved that I had a graphic design background and had sound knowledge of the things I was talking about. I moved to Sydney, which I grew to love, and I hosted the show for a year and a half.

For the first time in my life, I began to look after myself with a passion. I finally had my dream job and it inspired me to look after myself well. I wanted to keep that hosting role and have the energy to do well at it. The attention from the job made me bloom rather than wilt, which is what would have happened when my thinking was so negative and depressive. I was now eating well and exercising to help me be strong, not to lose weight. The job made me feel good and I finally felt I deserved to do and be well. When *CyberShack* ended, I decided that with all my life experiences, I would be good at acting and I enrolled at the National Institute of Dramatic Art and did some amazing classes. I learned so much and found new ways to express myself.

I've just been cast in a film and had a guest role on *Packed to the Rafters*, which was a great experience. In my classes I learned how to make everything I had experienced work for me as an actor. I have felt the gamut of human emotions in my life and I now know I can use that to bring me strength and life. I have acted in some advertisements and a show on the Comedy Channel called *Balls of Steel* too, and now acting is something I want to do full time, using myself as a canvas for people's stories.

I have been seeing a spiritual healer for some time and he has been teaching me about acceptance of myself and how to be more aware of my thoughts. Learning how to be really present and honouring the moment has helped me to heal my inner child. I no longer feel like a lost little girl who has to be told she is OK. I know I can do that for myself now. I have learned to become my own inner parent and nurture myself with love from within. I feel like now is my time.

Throughout my recovery I wrote a great deal and kept a journal. This creative release through writing as well as drawing and making things was a lifeline for me. I don't feel as if there was one big thing that got me through my illness, more a succession of little things. The car ride after my escape from Wagga hospital with Paul was certainly a pivotal moment, as it acted like a reality check after the horrible time I'd had in hospital. It was the first time I was able to focus on my recovery and learn to eat again. I couldn't pretend anymore.

I truly believe that what you focus on magnifies and that includes your thoughts. By moving away from negative thoughts and towards developing more positive ones, you in turn grow into a more positive life force yourself. I know some people say they like to fight their eating disorder, but for me it was never about fighting, rather choosing more positive things to focus on. Instead of fighting and pushing back against the eating disorder, which I think is draining, I learned to accept that it was there and I believe that took away its power.

I thought about my eating disorder from the perspective of trying to find out what it was telling me about me and my life and asking questions as to why it had come to me. I have come to the conclusion that I developed an eating disorder because I was not focusing on enough positivity and self-love. I wasn't treating myself well and putting myself first. In many ways, it was even a sign that I was not being fed what I needed to thrive and be happy, hence my issues with food.

I live a much more realistic, grounded and centred life now and I'm no longer floating about like that tissue in the wind. I have an internal well of balance and power and this helps me to deal with any feelings of stress or potential triggers. I have to be careful to not take on the emotions or troubles of others too much as I know that, because I'm a very empathetic person, I can fall into others' issues if I'm not wary. Things will always challenge me but the best thing I can do is choose to be aware of my thinking and catch anything that I know is not serving me well.

Despite all of the horrible things that have happened to my family, we are now united by an unconditional love. Without that, I'm certain that Phoebe, Doug and I would not love one another as we do today and would have had very different reactions to our terrible losses. My family, especially my mum and dad, has taught me that we must love people for who they are despite their flaws. The compassion and understanding I have for others is a gift I got from them and I will always be grateful for that.

Learning to love them as they were, and my brother, sister and nephews, pulled me through my darkest times. Because of them I have been able to find the most important ingredient for my healing, which is self-love. I had to learn to unconditionally love myself before any of the love around me could get in. And there was a lot there, even though I sometimes mistook it for chaos.

I am proud of and love the family I have come from. All of them have taught me about love, loss and life in a way that I may never have experienced if born and raised in different circumstances. That's certainly something to be enormously grateful and positive for, which I am every day.

Ally's Recovery Tips

1. Surround yourself with positivity. Be it a friend, family member, pet or an object that brings you comfort, try to find joy in something outside of yourself until you can find it inside yourself. My cat brought me so much love and I enjoyed collecting crystals and learning about their healing properties.
2. Let love in! Accept the love that your friends and family offer. Fill up your tank and feel the difference love makes.
3. Always remember you are not your thoughts. With practice, you can choose to let negative thoughts pass you by and choose to believe positive ones. Begin by observing your thoughts and seeing what they are telling you. I know I have thoughts that belong to 'Betty Beat Up' or 'Stella Storyteller' that aren't mine. I just say, 'Thanks, Betty, for sharing, but no thanks', and the impact of harsh thinking passes me by.

4. Get creative! Having an outlet for expressing your feelings is a great tool to get them out of your head and onto paper, canvas or whatever you choose. Sing, play an instrument, or take some arty photos. Write a fictional story about your secret dream life. I enjoyed making dream catchers for friends, drawing and sewing. Artistic expression makes way for positivity and new ways of seeing the amazing world we're living in.

5. Even though you may feel dark, remember you have the power to choose a new feeling at any time. Focus on the light, not the darkness. Take a moment each day to tell yourself positive affirmations – 'I let the love in' is a personal favourite. You begin to believe what you repeat, so any negative beliefs you have learned you can 'un-learn' and replace with more helpful ones.

Daydream Believer

Solveig's Story

Anyone could be forgiven for thinking that Solveig has lived not one life, but many. She has lived in many countries and had successful careers in both straight-size and plus-size modelling, journalism and as a Pilates instructor. Her greatest achievement, however, has been overcoming an eating disorder and post-traumatic stress disorder, testament to her stay at an inpatietnt clinic, counselling and her own willpower and strength.

I was born in Germany, the only child of my parents' marriage. I grew up with an older half-sister from my father's previous marriage and later, two younger half-siblings when Mum remarried. Despite this, I never felt I belonged to a family unit. As a little girl I loved daydreaming and making up my own special worlds. I was a loner by necessity. I would make up stories and songs and I read voraciously. Daydreaming was special to me, but it was also the bubble I created for myself as a way to cope with my parents' failing marriage and, later, my emotionally abusive mother.

My relationship with my parents was difficult. I remember them fighting viciously and one of my most vivid memories is being woken up in the middle of the night and waiting for a cab in my PJs with Mum, who was telling me how bad Dad was. When they separated, she projected her anger towards me. Dad became very absent from my life after I lived with Mum, and I only saw him twice from when I was eight until I was sixteen.

When I was six, Mum introduced me to my step-father. He tried to be nice to me but he was awkward with kids and I resented him. I probably felt threatened he would take Mum, the only person I was close to, away from me. We moved to a new town two years later and I lost all my other close ties: my grandmothers, who would look after me after school and who I adored, my friends and my older sister. My baby sister was born and while I loved her with my whole heart, my isolation deepened. They were now a family I was not a part of. When my brother was born, this feeling intensified. I often thought that one day my real parents would turn up and that I must have been switched when I was a baby in hospital. I thought there had to be a family out there who liked the things I did and who missed me, because I constantly felt like an outsider.

As a small girl I had recurring middle ear infections. I was given a lot of antibiotics to treat the condition, but they destroyed the good bacteria in my system and I developed allergies to a variety of foods. Caring for me when I was sick was a way for Mum to express affection. I was put on different elimination diets to try to work out what I could safely eat. I resented being on them but at this time I also loved school and my teachers. I was naturally good at most subjects but I still never felt good enough. I never felt loved. To cope, I would retreat inside the worlds I created in my head and I started writing books, drawing and painting. Being creative, along with reading, helped me enormously. It allowed me to bring the beautiful world I was imagining out onto paper and into the real world.

Signs of my eating disorder began to surface from when I was about twelve. Mum had been strict about food to the point of me not being allowed to take anything from the fridge unless I asked. It was considered very rude to get something to eat without everyone in the family being offered some too. And while I was a conforming and respectful do-gooder on the outside, I would sometimes sneak down to the basement freezer to have an ice-cream. The problem was, I often couldn't stop at one and would eat lots at once. It soon became a compulsive behaviour. I also wasn't allowed to have breakfast on weekends before anyone else did. I was an early riser, awake long before everyone else in my family got up, but all I could do was set the table and then wait for hours for others to rise.

My allergies became worse and going through puberty also scared me. I didn't have a strong female role model and no one ever spoke to me about the changes I was going through. When I got my period, I freaked out and cried. Despite my feelings and everything that was happening in my family, life certainly wasn't all bad. I continued to love school and had great friends. I was also passionate about sports and I did gymnastics, yoga, dance, fencing, badminton and basketball and loved them all.

When I was sixteen, I got my first boyfriend. He was a gorgeous boy and we had a great relationship. It shone a different light onto my family; I saw how another family was and realised not everything in my home was normal. It made me think about my dad and I wondered if everything Mum was telling me about him was true. I wanted to contact him and move out of home but Mum forbade me, saying I would be disowned if I did. Things came to a head when my boyfriend left to go to Australia on an exchange. We were very in love and he didn't want to break up, but I knew it was a wonderful opportunity and I wanted him to do it without missing me. As soon as he left I became incredibly sad and lost without him.

I did go and see Dad and my older half-sister, but it felt very unsettling and I quickly realised I had a lot of trust issues with him that were unresolved. I also realised he was not nice to my sister and I didn't want that for myself. By now I was seventeen and Mum and my stepfather told me they wanted me to leave home. I got a share flat with some young people, and while on one hand I was relieved to be out, on the other I was incredibly angry that I was kicked out when not long before I had wanted to leave on my own terms.

Just prior to moving out of home I'd started to do some modelling. I had always loved acting and drama at school and a wide variety of people told me I should model. My older sister told me modelling could help with my acting, which piqued my interest. But it was a bad choice for me at the time. I hated the way I looked, was very awkward, and had low self-esteem. I contacted some agencies, the first of which told me to lose ten kilograms and come back. The second agency told me I had to lose three kilograms, giving me instructions on what foods to cut from my diet. I cut out not only the foods they recommended, but more, and I lost more weight than they told me to. It was the start of my spiral into uncontrollably disordered eating.

As soon as I lost weight, I had several shoots and appeared on TV and in a music video, but instead of feeling validated by it, and despite others telling me it was terrific, I felt awful. I was scrutinised in castings and felt like nothing more than a clothes hanger. The industry made me feel like I wasn't a person. I would go to castings and shoots and people would ask me if I had put on weight or tell me that something didn't look good on me. It was very confronting. I was sent out to please people but had no control over how to do it.

I only modelled for a few months. Since beginning to diet, my inner world had become populated with even more self-hatred and scrutiny. I started to obsess about food and became compulsive about exercise. My eating spiralled out of control and my school attendance fell away. I was crying a great deal and swinging between bingeing, dieting and exercising compulsively. I had an eating disorder but didn't know it.

I would go to the supermarket and buy food but within hours of arriving home I had devoured it all. I was trying to fill up and smother or starve my feelings, but it wasn't working. Food had become my drug. I kept functioning – just – and no one knew anything was wrong, even though inside I felt like I was dying. I kept up a brave face, which I had now been doing my entire life, but deep down I knew I needed help. I went to see a counsellor twice but they tried hypnosis on me, which triggered a panic attack when the counsellor sent me back to the age of three. I never went back.

By now I regularly felt suicidal. I was barely hanging on and I would stay in bed for days in a dark room. I had no control over food and I thought everything that was happening to me was my fault. I had been told I was bad since I was old enough to remember, so thinking any other way seemed impossible. The hurt became so bad I knew I needed professional help. A friend recommended a good doctor and I opened up to her. She diagnosed me with an eating disorder and referred me to a specialist clinic.

I had to stay there for a minimum of two months and would be allowed no contact with the outside world for the first two weeks. By now I felt like it was my only hope. I counted the days down to my admission. Weeks felt like years. I was burdened with so much pain. It hurt to think and eating or starving myself had become the drug that numbed my mind and body. I hated myself and was desperate for help.

The clinic was amazing and going there was the best decision I could have made. There were individual, group and creative therapies, which helped me enormously. We had a nutritionist and we did physical therapy and went on two gentle walks a day. I saw other girls starve themselves, abuse their bodies and despair, and it made me fight for my sanity. I stayed for nine weeks and when I left I moved into a flat with a friend. I felt much better but I wasn't fully recovered. I went back to school after a summer break and took things slowly. It was a better year than the one before and I had good friends who supported me.

My eating was much calmer, but still compulsive at times. I was hyper aware of not wanting to lose control and felt I had to be vigilant about my emotions to try to make sure I didn't spin out. I preferred to eat too much rather than too little, a practice that continued for a number of years. I also still had to stop myself from exercising at times. I was worried anything would turn into an addiction. Throughout my final year I also saw a great counsellor regularly. The thing they helped me with most was the anger I felt towards Mum.

I enrolled to study French and politics at university but changed to a triple diploma in languages to prepare me to work for the foreign office. The study was initially based in England but I quickly realised that with my solid grasp of all the languages already, I wasn't learning anything new. I was devastated to be paying so much for a course that wasn't teaching me anything.

I began seeing a sweet guy and fell pregnant to him while I was sick with a severe kidney infection. I had to take strong medication for the infection and was told the drugs I had been taking would potentially be detrimental to my baby's development. I was positive about being a mum and initially made the decision to continue with the pregnancy, but the more I learned about the side effects of the medication and being told my baby was likely to be born with a serious disability, I made the heartbreaking decision to have an abortion.

It was a shocking experience. I did not want to kill the life that was growing inside me and I woke up from the anaesthetic crying. I got an infection and felt incredibly guilty about what I had done. I tried making peace with myself but throwing myself into work was the only escape I could find.

I'd given up my studies and was temping in London when the reality of what I'd done hit me six months later. My relationship with my boyfriend suffered and I tried to see a counsellor but was told I would have to wait a year before being able to see anyone. When counselling was made impossible I knew I had to pick myself up and make a commitment to get on with my life. I started working with an IT recruitment company and quickly became very good at my job. During this time, I broke up with my boyfriend. The abortion had hit us hard. I did what I knew worked best for me – walled myself in and got on with things.

About a year into my job, I was working long hours and was very unbalanced. From the outside I looked successful but I felt very empty inside and I woke up one morning and felt like I couldn't move or function. I went on a holiday and realised my life was nothing like what I would have chosen freely. I had never wanted to work in recruitment and felt that if given a choice, writing was my calling. I'd just been too worried about failure to admit it to myself. I felt as if Australia may be a great place for me to try, especially as I had some friends from there who kept telling me I would fit in well with the lifestyle.

I moved to Sydney at age twenty-four and started plus-size modelling. I wanted to use the money to pay for a journalism degree. I had heard about plus-size modelling and it felt like a second chance for me. I was now more comfortable in my body despite having gained weight due to an ankle injury and being unable to exercise. I was still eating more than I truly felt comfortable with to keep the eating disorder at bay, but I signed with an agency and in my first week I was in *Cosmopolitan* magazine.

I was a success right from the start and it felt different for me this time because I was older and more sure of myself. I didn't feel the pressure I previously had. I got in touch with my old agency in Germany and booked international work with them too. Things were going really well for me until I went to a modelling party where my drink was spiked and I was raped by several men. I was hit hard but the thought that a court case would prevent them from hurting anyone else pulled me through.

Two months after the rape I got booked for an overseas shoot, allowing me time away. When I returned, I fell for a genuinely loving and caring guy. Even though I was never fully sure of the relationship, I was swept away by his love for me and I agreed to get married. Life became a blur of overseas trips, jet lag, dealing with the police and wedding plans. But when I realised the police investigation into my case had stalled and I was told it was my word against theirs and I would not be able to give good evidence because I was drugged, everything came to a crashing halt.

I had been propelled forwards by wanting justice for what had happened to me and I also felt like it had happened to me for a reason, because I felt I could do something about it. Things came tumbling down when I knew I couldn't fight back. My fiancé and I started to fight, as he felt unable to help me and developed black and dark feelings himself. Hatred towards the attackers turned into anger against the police and disappointment with our society as a whole. I was barely functioning but we got married anyway. Almost a year after the rape, post-traumatic stress officially descended upon me. I began to have days where I didn't know what was real and what wasn't. The jetlag and moving between time zones was making me crazy and I felt like my whole life was invaded. I felt unsafe even taking a shower and crowded places like buses and malls freaked me out. The public prosecutor's office helped by putting me in touch with a counsellor.

It was months of daily struggle and then another year after that before I felt like I was in control again. My short term memory suffered. My body felt like it wasn't my own. I felt so black about the world and had suicidal thoughts so often that I gave up resisting, believing the best thing to do was to allow myself to feel them. I tempered the thoughts with the belief that if I wasn't one hundred per cent certain that ending my life was the best thing to do, then I could maybe hold on for another day, or another week, or another year. I gave myself permission and said it was OK, if I wanted to commit suicide, to take away its power, knowing that I didn't have to do it if I didn't want to. It diffused the feelings and stopped the need for me to do anything impulsive.

I got through by focusing intently on what I could do, bringing back normality with routines, one step at a time. I often thought back to my time at the eating disorder clinic and why I had made the decision to get well and move on with my life. I went for gentle walks every day, reclaimed showering as a nourishing and cleansing ritual and treated myself with as much kindness as possible.

My underlying resilience and positivity kicked in. I remember the moment I knew I was out the other side. I'd gone for a run and stood on a cliff near the ocean where a wave of gratitude came over me. I felt alive and utterly in awe of nature's beauty. I cried silent tears of joy all the way home and I knew in that moment I'd accepted myself more fully than I ever had before. I had looked into the abyss and come out alive. No one could take me away from me.

I didn't model for a while during recovery and when I started again I was a smaller size. By not keeping up my false sense of control around food, my body changed. I was now between a straight size and plus size, and it felt good to me. I had found my natural set weight. I'd begun to study journalism and did work experience at newspapers and a travel magazine. I was good at it and it helped me to come back to myself.

By this time my husband and I knew we had grown apart. I realised I had never been in a place where I was fully able to be in love with him. While I loved him, valued him and respected him as a friend, I could no longer be with him. I finished my journalism studies and worked for a major newspaper and magazine and found journalism and writing to be my calling. Telling stories and engaging with people was wonderful, but there was still some healing that was to come in my life.

The moment at the cliff was one of the first times I felt in my body again. The post-traumatic stress had numbed me and the eating disorder had made me feel incredible pain. I was more grounded in my body and from that moment on I felt like I had more flow in my life. It was like I was reborn. Previously, when my inner voice had criticised me, I had to make a very conscious decision to like myself. Now it felt so much more natural and for the first time in my life I truly believed I was an OK person. I didn't need anyone to validate me or prove anything to myself.

These last few years have been incredible for me and I have learned a lot from letting myself open up and fall in love with people who were ultimately wrong for me. One particularly challenging relationship helped me reconnect with myself on a level I never thought possible. I've learned to listen to my intuition and my inner voice, which I'd feared in my early twenties when it was difficult for me to distinguish it from my disordered thoughts. I've learned to trust and work with my body, knowing it will work in conjunction with my mind and soul, and ultimately protect me from harm. And I've learned about boundaries, mental hygiene and connecting with others on a meaningful level – all of which I feel my upbringing lacked.

This last year has been incredible for me. As well as writing, I am a Pilates instructor, which I love. The Pilates way of moving makes my body feel incredibly alive and I love teaching that to others. I firmly believe that any industry, including modelling, needs to accept me as I am. It's not healthy for any person to constantly be on a diet or eating in a way that is not balanced. I have made a promise to myself not to treat my body in that way anymore.

I have started a regular yoga and meditation practice and have become more spiritual, balanced and joyful. The wounds from my past are clearing from my body and I have moved away from counselling or talking to friends about my issues, instead taking my healing to a physical level. Allowing myself to face the pain that I held inside, without verbalising or intellectualising it, has bought an enormous shift in me. I have now learned on a very deep, spiritual and physical level that I don't have to fear anything.

Bringing together mind, body and spirit has become my main aim in life. I no longer sweat the small stuff and can laugh at challenges and silly mistakes. I am making peace with my family, those who have wronged me and those I do not like. I have learned to love myself and those around me on a deeper level not because I am wanting to or telling myself to, but because I'm feeling it. It's an amazing time to be me.

Solveig's Recovery Tips

1. While you might feel as if your whole world is shrouded in darkness, there is always light at the end of the tunnel. That light is actually the whole world waiting for you. It's wondrous and beautiful and amazing, and it's worth every step you take in recovery to get there.
2. Be forgiving of yourself, especially as your recovery path may see you take steps backwards and sideways, as well as forwards. Nothing in life is ever really that linear and if you beat yourself up for not doing well all the time, it will make things so much harder for you.
3. If you are reading this book and you are suffering, I know you can recover. The fact you are here means that your heart wants you to be happy and well.

4. Find little things that give you joy and help you, and do them or surround yourself with them often. It could be reading, a pet, gardening, gentle walking or a person who lifts you up. You deserve to have your life filled with these things, all which will help with your recovery.
5. Consider reading inspirational books as something that can open your mind to other people's stories of triumph, overcoming adversity, life experiences and personal wisdom. There is a great deal of truth and love in people's stories that can help to inspire you to wellness.

True Love

Hannah's Story

Hannah's passion and dedication to ballet saw her initially shine but later contributed to her becoming trapped in the torturous world of anorexia. Her life journey is punctuated with a deeply traumatic hospitalisation and years of self-loathing, but is now filled with a passion for life and living, supported by a pivotal meeting with a doctor and a deeply trusting relationship with a gifted psychologist.

For as long as I can remember, my childhood was spent lost in a creative world that was all my own. I was the youngest of four children and my family lived in a small country town in Victoria, where we were well known. My dad had returned to the western district to raise a family after a career as an elite footballer and professional reserves coach. As a sporty family, we were very much a part of the fabric of our town, which had a large football and netball culture. I was often referred to as 'the dancer', as I took a different path and was passionate about classical ballet from a young age.

I have fond memories of time spent creating adventures with my elder siblings on our farm, watching classic movies with my dearest grandmother, going to the footy with my father, and of the array of love and affection my mother showered upon me always. But amid this picture of perfection and this seemingly ideal family, a shadow was cast over my parents' marriage and, at the age of six, my family as I knew it was shattered and lost to me forever.

I watched as the thread that once bound my family together began to unravel. Although unable to understand the complexity of the situation at the time, I understood all too well that the five most influential figures in my life were suffering, especially as Dad moved to Melbourne shortly after he and Mum separated. As a child I had always been very sensitive to what other people were feeling, and I knew my leaving Mum to stay with Dad when he came to visit would devastate her further. This was an unnerving time for me and I found being away from Mum very difficult. I thought her feelings were very connected to my own and I experienced extreme anxiety when taken away from the person I felt the closest to at such a young, impressionable age.

It did not take long before my difficulties at home became difficulties at school. Ballet soon became my expressive outlet, my sanctuary, and the only place that really felt like home to me over the coming years. A former Australian Ballet soloist ran a school in town and I responded to her wonderful teaching as well as the discipline and challenge of dance. By the time I was eight years old, I had made a conscious decision to pursue a professional dancing career, and my determination and dedication was recognised by those around me. Although I trained in other styles, traditional ballet always remained my first love and was what I wanted to concentrate on most. The studio was a haven for me and I would go there at lunchtime to escape school, where I was being bullied. My dance teacher became my mentor and main influence as I began to retreat from those close to me. From the outside looking in, it appeared that it was my commitment to dancing that was the reason for my seclusion.

By late primary school, when most of my peers were going through puberty, I began to lose weight and a story of rigorous and relentless training of both my mind and body began to play out. The little girl in me slowly slipped away, and over the next few years was replaced by obtrusive obsessions and imperfections that I saw in everything around me and, most predominantly, in myself. Cleanliness had become a necessity just like my religion, a rigorous chore I had to uphold. Cleverly disguised, these activities all went unnoticed in our busy home and with each new victory of deception, a dark voice within became more persistent, more demanding and more consuming.

My weight loss attracted comments at school. Girls asked me how I was doing it and boys began to notice me. I distinctly remember a family friend highlighting that I now 'looked like a ballerina', which to me was the biggest compliment I could be paid. This was all happening at a time when I was excelling at dance and receiving encouragement and accolades for my achievements. While it may have appeared that I was succeeding, at school I continued to feel extremely ostracised. As the exclusionary bullying escalated, dance continued to be the only thing that offered me an escape from the outside world. At the end of primary school I wanted to take up the opportunity to attend the Australian Ballet summer school instead of our annual family camping holiday, which brought about my first point of conflict with Mum. By now she felt I was too immersed in dance and she had noticed my gradual weight loss. But I was determined to go. And I did.

I threw myself into the summer school and thrived off being in an environment that was home to some of Australia's best classical dancers and teachers. We were told that to be a professional dancer you had to maintain a certain physique, but I don't recall the school directly encouraging restrictive or dangerous behaviours. Despite this, I now found myself making the conscious decision to drastically restrict my food intake. I believed I needed to sustain my pre-pubescent body to remain part of the ballet world as, inside this exclusive environment and surrounded by towering mirror-clad walls and pictures of my idols, my insecurities seemed acceptable and understandable; my imperfections highlighted. It was the only space I felt remotely talented and safe in and I didn't want to do anything to jeopardise that. By the end of the summer school I undoubtedly had anorexia.

By now Mum was very concerned, especially as I was about to start high school. On my first day, I refused to take off my jumper even though it was summer. I was trying to hide my body and was often cold regardless of the temperature. Although I was retaining good grades and had found a teacher at school who was supportive and encouraging of my passion for the arts, by now I was very unwell and struggling to concentrate in class.

I continued to maintain my focus on dance but my ballet teacher had also expressed a concern about my now-rapid weight loss and was quietly watching at a safe but close distance. She was very careful about how she approached me, telling me she could see my dancing was improving but that she was worried about my health and wellbeing.

The sequence of events that followed was swift and powerful, and by the time it was obvious to family and friends what was occurring, I was already drowning within the confines of anorexia and depression. In the space of a year I had successfully withdrawn from everyone I loved, becoming a reclusive, secretive shadow of my former self. Many times I felt like I was not even conscious in my own body and had no idea what I was doing. Devastatingly, I felt I was not worthy of nourishment or of love.

After receiving a phone call from the concerned parent of someone I danced with, Mum went through my room in search of evidence that I was engaging in dangerous behaviours, which she found in numerous forms. As she was working as a medical receptionist at a clinic in town, she arranged for me to see one of the female doctors there. But the doctor had no experience with eating disorders and I was put on a high carbohydrate diet. I was extremely observant and distrustful of those around me and on one of my weekly visits I found Mum entering the weigh-in room after I left. I realised that my doctor was allowing Mum to view my records. The eating disorder immediately told me Mum had betrayed me and I completely withdrew from her.

With no other alternative, and with reservations on my father's behalf, my parents briefly reunited as joint guardians to embark on a mission to seek out the best possible care in the hope of recovering the daughter they had now lost. An appointment was made with a doctor at an adolescent centre in Melbourne. He was a young specialist known to be one of the best in his field. I still remember everything about that day: the date, the appointment time, the deathly silence in the car for the four hours it took to reach our final destination and the guilt I was now drenched in. Half an hour after my consultation, I was admitted to a children's hospital.

I was twelve years old when admitted to a general adolescent ward. The month I was there was the most traumatic of my life, and it was not until years later that I came to realise the experience left me with post-traumatic stress disorder. I had all of my belongings taken away from me and was restricted to bed rest as an incentive to try to encourage me to eat, but as I was now desperately homesick, this was even more difficult than before. Bathing was seen as one of many privileges that were taken away from me as I continued to lose weight, although even in such harsh surroundings I was given the nickname the 'Angelic Anorexic' by the medical staff, due to my placid and polite nature.

The decision was made to change me to a private hospital after it became evident I was not responding to treatment. I remember feeling almost excited at the prospect of meeting someone who might be able to offer an insight into what was happening to me, but when I found out I was seven years younger than all the other eating disorder patients I realised I still had no one to relate to. I now felt more alone and depressed than ever before, as I was deemed too young for group therapy and received only limited counselling.

I went from being monitored twenty-four hours a day to only being supervised during meal times. Desperate to return home, I opened up to Mum and Dad for the first time about how afraid and homesick I was. I promised them I would do everything in my power to get well if they allowed me to return home. Seeing my distress, they obliged. I left the private hospital at the same weight I was admitted at.

Returning home with no medical support or knowledge about the illness meant the next couple of years were tumultuous for both my family and me. I was prescribed an antidepressant and pretty much left to my own devices, with dancing once again becoming my only form of therapy. Out of sheer determination and fear of returning to hospital, I managed to put on small amounts of weight, a seemingly simple task that was indescribably difficult under watchful eyes.

After a matter of only months, I once again gave in to the voices of my eating disorder and stopped eating altogether. I was swinging wildly between having feelings of complete lunacy and catching myself and wondering if I was destined to disappear altogether. When I was eventually force fed by my parents, I became violently ill and I had to be taken to hospital, where I remained under strict supervision for three days, drifting in and out of consciousness. To this day, I do not know what happened during that time. The experience frightened me, although I was still unable to truly understand the severity of the situation or the damage I was doing to my mind and body.

Over the next twelve months I somehow managed to stabilise my weight as I continued with both school and dance. I transferred to a performing arts school in Melbourne for my final year, and by now I had accepted that I was never going to have a professional career as a classical ballerina. After the initial excitement of landing in a city where I was almost completely anonymous, as well as the prospect of doing something that I loved on a daily basis, reality slowly seeped in. At the performing arts school, I was once again surrounded by dangerous comparisons and negativity.

The teaching styles used at the school were never going to work for my fragile mind. I had come from the serenity and calm of the classic ballet world and didn't know how to handle the overt sexuality at the school. Dance was my one great passion and I felt completely lost. I lasted six months before transferring to a different performing arts school.

Luckily, I immediately fell in love with my new surroundings. With the support of both my peers and mentors, I truly blossomed as both a dancer and an individual. After graduating from the course, I accepted a place within the school's professional agency, launching a career as both a teacher and commercial dancer. I began to slowly build a number of strong friendships as well as invaluable experience within the industry.

It was also during this time that I fell in love for the first time. I had never allowed myself to be so vulnerable or close to another person and the relationship quickly developed into the most amazing connection, one that brought an intimacy to my life that I had never experienced. Although the relationship helped me to evolve as a person, I still felt as if the eating disorder was always waiting and watching me from the wings. I couldn't eat or drink anything without thinking about it both before and after and I was highly conscious of my body. I was dancing and exercising excessively, and my mind was a mix of constant irrational and rational thoughts. It was only the rational thoughts that allowed me to maintain the mask of a young woman with a promising career and enviable romance.

Twelve months into my relationship, I was given the opportunity to dance as a soloist on a cruise ship in the USA. Believing my relationship was strong enough to last the distance and time apart, I accepted the role. It was an arduous job where I was weighed every week by the dance captain. Although I continued to maintain appearances, this invasive and restrictive environment saw those around me become aware of my excessive behaviours, and a combination of triggers saw the worst side of my eating disorder surface again – and to its full capacity. I felt desperately lonely and isolated as the future I had planned began to slip out of my grasp.

By the time I returned home I had lost a lot of weight, something that shocked and angered my partner. I immediately knew that my eating disorder would be my secret no more, and I finally confessed to the relentless and obsessive thoughts and behaviours that had haunted me for years. It was a devastating blow to what was meant to be the start of our life together. In the months that followed, and as I embarked on a mission to get well, it became obvious that our relationship, no matter how special, was not going to survive my personal journey of recovery. I also made the heartbreaking decision to stop dancing, finally realising I needed to focus on getting well.

Relieved that I had finally asked for help after all these years, Mum rang the Butterfly Foundation in search of a referral and I was sent to a specialising GP. I instantly felt comfortable in his presence and divulged everything, in an enthusiastic attempt to 'get well'. At the end of my appointment the GP told me he couldn't help me, and I collapsed on his consulting room floor. Although I had always refused to play the victim, I was beginning to think that I would die like this, and for the first time in years I allowed myself to completely fall apart. As the doctor gently picked me up, he encouraged me to meet with a psychologist he worked closely with. Having no other alternative, I weakly agreed.

The psychologist he referred me to changed my life. She garnered my trust by moving slowly and, over time, helped to tear down the eating disorder while building me up. With an interest in holistic treatment, together we worked on rebuilding a positive mind–body relationship. I found her at the right time for me, and I became diligent about getting well. I realised that if I could focus so intently on something as negative as hating myself, I could flip that into focusing on liking myself and hating the eating disorder. I also met someone who was to become one of my dearest friends, a woman who had recovered from an eating disorder. She spoke about full recovery as something that was an absolute possibility, which only further instilled in me the desire to be free.

I saw the psychologist regularly over two years, along with occasional appointments with a dietician and GP. It was a challenging, all-encompassing journey that was extremely difficult, but had amazing moments of self-discovery. Through treatment, I learned to practice yoga and meditation, which have remained a passion of mine and a wonderful life skill. I did return to dance classes for a while but I realised it was too much of a triggering environment for me and I acknowledged that this would not be an ongoing career. I had to see it as a love that had now ended and move on. It brought out such perfectionism in me, I realised I had to leave it behind to truly become well.

Throughout this time I also rebuilt relationships with my family, as I was now slowly allowing the barriers around me to be destroyed. Tests on my body had shown the eating disorder had done a lot of damage and I was told that I may struggle to have children, something that I had always desired. I wanted to reverse the damage to my mind and body and once I found the team to help me, as well as the unwavering support of a wonderful friend and family, there was no turning back.

I experience bad body image days like everyone else but they are realistic now, and I feel this is a representation of the perfectly imperfect individual I am today. I am, at times, in awe of how free I now feel around food and how blessed I am to be alive and well. In many ways, I feel like I have been reborn and am starting afresh, with my life just beginning in my twenties. Although I acknowledge that I have lost a great deal to the eating disorder, it pales in comparison to the life and opportunities I now harness. I have gained a wonderful sense of self-awareness and assurance and I see life as a beautiful gift. There were times that were so bleak that I wanted to give up the fight, something I know I will never feel again. I now have the skills to heal myself and to help stop that from happening.

I proudly worked as a project officer for the Butterfly Foundation in education and awareness for over three years – something I couldn't do unless I was one hundred per cent well in both body and mind – and have now returned home to southwest Victoria, where I continue to advocate for positive self-esteem and community engagement with youth. My illness has clearly lead me into this line of work but I wouldn't do it if I wasn't truly passionate about my job.

If anything makes me feel anxious or uncomfortable for an extended period of time, I remove myself from its path. Life's too short for intense and desperate emotions and I've already lost too much time. I am very connected with my family and even though the eating disorder nearly tore us apart, it has also played a key role in bringing us closer. I spent many years investing in and building the most amazing friendships and support network, which I am now so grateful for. I have a rich tapestry of relationships and feel ready for a partner whenever this presents itself. My desire is to lead a simple and happy life, not one that requires me to be perfect or overtly ambitious.

Incredible people played a very significant role in my recovery. From a healing perspective, my psychologist and my mentor were pivotal, but I am also extremely grateful to my ballet teacher, who I believe kept me alive to an extent and connected me to something throughout those chaotic years. She was able to reach me at my darkest moments, and later the psychologist helped to nurture the child in me that was lost, which enabled me to feel like a whole person again.

I know what it is like to be in a place of such darkness that you don't know what could possibly pull you through, but I am certain that connections with these people helped me to do just that. All three, in their own way, built me up to realise that my one true love in life was not dance. It's me.

Hannah's Recovery Tips

1. It is worth searching for the right professional or professionals who can help you. There is someone out there for you who can help and if you haven't found them, keep searching.
2. Your life is a gift but it will only feel like it if you are truly free of your eating disorder and able to live and breathe every moment as your own person. Believe in yourself enough to know that your life can feel like a gift if you continue to focus on being well.
3. A mentor who has recovered from an eating disorder can be a powerful ally in you getting well. Seek out someone who can inspire you with their own journey to wellness and the belief that recovery is possible for everyone.

4. Explore new things that help bring about increased levels of self-awareness and enlightenment in your life. Consider doing some travel and exploring the arts to open up your heart and mind to new experiences.

5. Holistic therapies that can do wonders in helping you reach into your heart and soul to assist with your healing. Consider trying things such as massage, yoga and meditation as great additions in your wellness kit to recovery.

Beauty and Colour

Anna's Story

A dynamic and successful fashion designer, Anna's experience of anorexia saw a number of her teenage years shrouded in darkness, conflict and isolation. Hers is a story that shows how a positive connection with even just one treating professional, in this case a dietician, can make an incredible difference to someone's eating disorder recovery.

I grew up in the tiny township of Gol Gol, just over the New South Wales–Victoria border, for the first eleven years of my life, until my family moved to a property out of town. Dad was a wheat farmer and we shifted into our newly built home to be closer to the farm. I loved the space and being surrounded by bushland. My sister and I would make fairy gardens and collect broken china that had been buried there years before. I was the middle child of five and especially close to my sister, who was only eighteen months older than me. I loved going to the local primary school and my best friend lived only a short bike ride down the road on a grape block.

Despite loving primary school, I found myself anxious about starting high school. Coomealla High School was a big yellow-brick compound. It took students from all the country primary schools in the district, and was a half-hour bus trip from home. I remember being very scared of getting older and I felt sick about going into year seven. I was concerned about what would happen with my close friendships and how I would manage to make new friends or fit in with a bigger group.

Mum told me everything would be fine moving into year seven and it was. I still had my best friends from primary school and began making new friends, eventually forming a wonderful group of girls to hang out with. I was a bit of a drifter, though. Being athletic, I hung around the 'jock' crowd on sports days, but mainly stuck to my arty and academic circle of friends.

Despite this, my transition into high school slowly saw me develop a different attitude towards food. I remember in year six I would eat pies and sauce on Fridays, followed by a chocolate bar from the local store without a second thought. High school, along with a new bunch of girlfriends, brought about a new awareness of watching what we all ate, talk of dieting and a self-consciousness about eating in front of boys.

Not far into year eight, my parents decided to help a man who needed support and he and his two young children moved into our home. It was meant to last only until they found their feet but they ended up staying for two years. Looking back, I remember those years as being very dark for me. I struggled with the feeling that Mum was spending all her time and efforts ensuring the man and his two kids were OK. Dad became angry, blaming Mum for everything, struggling to deal with the situation he had put his family in. I believe my parents took the family in with good intentions, but it ended up being a nightmare situation.

Relationships were tested and my siblings and I were supposed to be 'grown up' about bearing a burden, instead of enjoying our younger years. I began to feel totally displaced in my own home and resented the fact that, on numerous occasions, I was reprimanded by my parents for ignoring the family. I did the only thing I knew how at the time: I threw myself into my school work, mostly so it would take up all my time and I would have an excuse to stay locked in my room and not see anyone. I was angry, upset and confused, and felt like I had been shoved aside. The only way I could cope was to crawl into a hole. I withdrew completely from my family and even started distancing myself from my sister.

Slowly but surely I turned away from food. I don't remember deliberately doing it, but after a comment from one of Mum's friends that I had 'a bit of a double chin', I made a conscious decision to get rid of that 'problem', despite the fact I had always been tall and thin with no sign of a double chin. By chance, I found a magazine from the '80s in Mum's room that had neck exercises in it and I did these religiously in the bathroom while getting ready for school. The more I obsessed I became over my neck, the more I became self-conscious of my twelve-year-old body, finding other areas that needed 'fixing'. My morning routine consisted of neck exercises and sit-ups behind closed doors to the point that I developed calluses on my spine.

I started to lose weight rapidly and began rigorous training for the cross-country race that was coming up later in the year. I also began throwing away my lunch at school. My family began to take notice, asking if I was OK. At one point my older brother demanded I not go for a run saying, 'Your legs look like toothpicks, Anna! What the hell are you training for?' This sudden attention felt like I was getting in trouble, but it was also nurturing. It gave me a place in the family because they were concerned about me. Only recently, my father told me that during this time I had a keen interest in cooking and preparing meals for everyone. It was the perfect cover to hide the fact that I wasn't eating myself.

I continued to throw away my lunch and refused to take part in meal times. One of my teachers, who was also my best friend's mother, asked me one day at lunchtime if I was OK. I told her to 'piss off and leave me alone' which was totally out of character for me. I began pushing my friends aside, hanging out with another group instead. My hands started turning purple in the cold and my skin became cracked and painful. I began doing all my classwork by the heaters in the classroom.

I remember one of my friends gave me a hug and while it felt nice to be hugged, it was even nicer for me to I feel how tiny my frame was in comparison to hers. I was becoming sicker, and at my lowest point I found myself in front of Dad's gun cabinet, a nasty little voice inside my head telling me I had to end my life. I had eaten more than I should that day and broken my own rules. I have no idea what saved me that day, but I am still sickened to think that the eating disorder had such an incredibly powerful grip on my life at the time.

One day, Dad burst into my room and demanded to know why I was throwing my lunch out. I flatly denied throwing anything out and slammed the door in his face. By the end of the week he had dragged me to a doctor's office to find a solution, reassuring me it was 'just a check-up', until the doctor started asking me questions about my eating habits. I refused to cooperate with the doctor, feeling angry and betrayed that my parents had gone behind my back and set up the appointment.

Many of my appointments from then on are a blur. I recall lots of blood tests and sending the doctor on a wild-goose chase, lying about my symptoms and hoping they would find that I had some strange unknown disease. I was in complete denial that I had an eating disorder. I was sitting in the clinic with Mum, awaiting test results, when the doctor said to me in a no-nonsense voice that I had anorexia nervosa. I felt shattered. There was nothing I could do. No more pretending. I had to face the fact that I was sick. All I could do was cry.

By this stage I had stopped going to school. Mum and Dad were keeping me at home and making sure I was getting the best possible treatment. The appointments kept coming and I started seeing a dietician. Karen had big brown eyes and a kind, calming voice. She was an incredible find. With her, I wasn't a hopeless head case and my illness wasn't a big deal. She was patient and explained things in detail in a way that encouraged me to trust her. I visited her twice a week and slowly she introduced the concept of putting on weight. I was petrified. Putting on weight meant I would lose control of yet another situation. I took everyone's comments about how thin I had become as compliments, and I think I thrived on the fact that everyone was concerned for my health. To gain weight would take that away and I would become invisible again.

My grandparents took me on a holiday to Canberra to visit my cousins, which would end up as a turning point in my recovery. Grandpa treated me as an adult. He told me he wasn't fussed if I ate or I didn't eat. It was my holiday and I could do what I pleased. This lack of surveillance and pressure must have had a profound effect on me as I remember sneakily eating Nutella from my cousin's kitchen when no one was around. The behaviour was still odd, but slowly the fear of fat was leaving me.

When we returned from Canberra, Grandma had our holiday happy snaps developed. I was horrified at myself. I was frail, white with sunken eyes, and only the faintest of smiles. I tore up those photographs in disgust and there are now no photographs of me during my illness at all. I can now understand that when you are ill, you can't see yourself how others see you. The whole image isn't seen in the mirror, only compartments of your body and areas that you focus on and obsess over.

Karen continued to work with me and gradually helped turn my life around. Over the Christmas holidays that year I was cooperating, putting on weight and becoming more sociable. By the time I began year nine, I had put on enough weight that people responded and told me I looked a thousand times better. Boys started to notice me and I felt my laughter returning. I stopped getting told I looked like Wednesday Addams, something a boy always teased me about because I was so pale and had sunken eyes.

There were still problems at home, however, and every night after school I would shrink into an angry, sullen teenager who couldn't stand having her home invaded by this extra, troubled family. One day after an appointment, sitting in a café, Mum asked me if there was anything about the situation at home that was upsetting me or making me want to stay ill. I lied. In that moment I had Mum all to myself and that was all I needed, but I said, no, it's totally fine, it's just me. To this day I wish I had been brave enough to be honest.

Over time, I tried to become more accepting of the situation and my sister and I actually became quite close to the girl that grew up with us. I realise now those young children would have felt just as out of place in my home as I did, and they weren't to blame. Eventually they moved out, but the negativity and tension lingered in our house long after they were gone, and by the time I finished high school I just wanted to move out of home.

As much as I appeared to be physically recovered in year nine, I still had a lot of emotional healing to go through. I was stronger, but had extremely low self-esteem, which would take many years to build. A kind comment from my grandma about how well I was looking had me paranoid I was overweight. I had a boyfriend during year nine, which I was excited about, but couldn't cope with the pressure of how to act around him in public. I was an awkward little thing and ended up breaking up with him after a week.

At the end of year ten I was frustrated with Coomealla High School and I moved to a new school in Mildura, where I was given better creative opportunities. I immersed myself in textiles, painting and sketching, and dabbled in chemistry and business. I loved the fresh start and met a bunch of amazing girls and started getting a lot of attention from boys. Life was better. I felt more in control of myself and more confident, although I still remember negative thoughts lurking below the surface. I achieved amazing results in my final exams and started dating the cutest boy I had ever met – Brett. Nine years later we have two businesses together, are newly married, and planning our future.

After my final year of school, I studied visual arts and then moved to Melbourne to study interior design. I loved it, but after two years I realised that it was lacking the colour and tactility I was seeking. Brett and I were in a long-distance relationship and I welcomed an excuse to move to Adelaide to be closer to him. I signed a leave of absence from university and moved to Glenelg, a small and calming suburb by the ocean. I absolutely loved my time there and then moved to the gorgeous Barossa Valley to work at a winery and save for a trip to Spain.

Spain became one of my biggest passions. It is so vibrant and alive with so much amazing culture and food. I developed a love affair with every city I visited. I was alone and backpacked around for three months. I arrived home brown as a nut with a fresh, inspired attitude to life. I didn't sign back into my course, instead completing a two-year TAFE course, learning, living and breathing fashion. Those two years have been some of the best of my life. While studying, I enjoyed work experience with Melbourne designer Helen Manuell and was working part time as an assistant to the designers at Pilgrim. By the time I had graduated I knew in my heart that I was going to start my own label and it was going to be called Violet & I.

I launched my first collection, Open Road, in spring 2009 and since then have continued to design and launch two major collections each year. I was in tears most of the time while I tried to sell my first collection. The knockbacks seemed constant and I was disheartened until someone pointed out to me that twelve stockists was amazing for a new label, especially considering we were in the worst financial climate of a long time. My style is very bohemian and free spirited and inspired by vintage pieces I collect from time to time. Hand drawing each collection and colouring them in is one of my favourite processes.

I love being surrounded by bursts of colour and silks that drape and flow effortlessly. I am inspired by so many things in life, including old photographs that I collected at Spanish flea markets and a stack of 1970s *Vogue* magazines, which I adore. My muses are fresh-faced beauties like Helena Christensen and Jade Jagger, and I'll often find myself even loving the headscarf or colourful cardigan on an old lady. Colour is a vital part of my designing process. I collect paint chips and scraps of coloured silk and line them up, rearranging them until I have my perfect colour palette each season.

I am a firm believer that everything happens for a

reason. If I hadn't become sick all those years ago, I am sure I would have breezed through high school without a care in the world. I would never have met the beautiful friends I did, I would not have met Brett, and I certainly wouldn't have the empathy I do for people suffering from eating disorders. In the back of my mind, I have always wanted to help others who have gone through, or are going through, an eating disorder, and Violet & I is now a sponsor of the Butterfly Foundation, which is a wonderful foundation that wasn't around when I was ill. With each collection I design, I give a percentage to the foundation to help fund the work they do. My goal is to raise awareness of eating disorders within the fashion industry and the wider community. Eating disorders can ruin and even end lives, but they didn't ruin mine and they don't need to ruin the next person's.

Working in an industry where there is so much expectation on looks, size and perfection, I am very mindful to support and use healthy-looking models in all my photo shoots. In a world where every glossy cover screams out at us to get this body or get that body, to lose baby weight overnight or to announce that curves are back in, I want Violet & I to be a label that every girl can love, wear and be a part of. I want Violet & I to encourage girls to be themselves and be confident.

It's often the little things we can do that make the most difference, as I learned when involved in a fashion show during Melbourne Spring Fashion Week. One of the organisers came running up to me, frantically telling me there was an issue with a model wearing one of my garments. She told me that the model's bum was too big for a pair of silk knickers, which actually wasn't the case at all. The model was a beautiful and healthy size and looked amazing, and I told her so. This misconception of size and beauty is a common problem, and trigger, in the fashion industry. There needs to be more focus on embracing diversity rather than freaking out that people don't fit the 'mould'. Whose mould is it anyway?

I love my creative and colourful life, and believe the professional help I received was very important in my recovery process. I was lucky to find someone I had a great connection with, who didn't expect anything of me until I was ready. I now value the concern my family showed, the strength they offered and the support I received from my circle of friends. When you are in the throes of an eating disorder, you are a feeble shadow of the person other people know you can be, and this often pushes friends and family aside. I was so lucky to have my family and friends stand by me and help me get well. I am incredibly close with my family now, especially Mum and my sister. I feel blessed to have left all the pain and struggling of my younger years in the past and am enjoying a bright and promising future.

People have told me there is no such thing as a full recovery, but to me that's not true. I feel fully recovered and have a great sense of self that has come with time, patience and self-belief. I think that recovery is truly possible for everyone, whatever it may look or feel like for each person. I am someone who manages my life, not an eating disorder. I believe recovery is when you can move on from negative thoughts and feelings and not get sucked into a tumbling darkness. It means for me that recovery is a world full of beauty and colour.

Anna's Recovery Tips

1. While it may seem hard for you to believe, life is waiting for you and you are allowed to do anything you like! Don't wait for life to come and choose you. The only restrictions you have are the ones you place on yourself, and working towards your recovery will help you understand that you do have choices. You will start living with every step you take towards getting well.
2. Professional help is a vital part of overcoming an eating disorder and a big part of this is the connection you feel to the person supporting you. There is someone, or even many people, who is right for you, who will make you feel safe and challenge the eating disorder at the same time. If you are in a country town, ensure you explore every option. Don't settle for a professional you don't feel is right.
3. An eating disorder tries to pull you away from everything and everyone you love and feel connected to, so trying to hold on to things you love is important. Doing things you love is at the heart of your true purpose, so do all you can to focus on them rather than your eating disorder.
4. Travel is a wonderful thing to do to help you expand your horizons and see the world from a whole new perspective. There are so many things waiting for you to touch, see, explore and taste,

that can make you feel more alive and inspired than you ever thought possible.

5. At the heart of many, if not all, eating disorders, is an identity crisis. When you're wrapped in its darkness, it can feel like it is taking away your authenticity but that is never truly possible. Your authentic self is always there and the way to return to it is to find and do what gives you purpose, making you feel alive and truly yourself.

Australian and International Eating Disorders Directory

International

Eating Disorders Actionist Network (EDAN)
www.edactivistnetwork.org
The Academy for Eating Disorders (AED)
www.aedweb.org
Families Empowered and Supporting Treatment of Eating
    Disorders (FEAST)
www.feast-ed.org

Australia

National

The Butterfly Foundation
www.thebutterflyfoundation.org.au
National Eating Disorders Collaboration
www.nedc.com.au

New South Wales

The Centre for Eating and Dieting Disorders (CEDD)
www.cedd.org.au

Queensland

Eating Disorders Association Inc Queensland
www.eda.org.au
ISIS: The Eating Issues Centre
www.isis.org.au

South Australia

Panic and Anxiety, Obsessive Compulsive and Eating Disorders
Associations (ACEDA)
www.aceda.org.au

Tasmania

Tasmania Recovery from Eating Disorders (TRED)
www.tred.org.au

Western Australia

Women's Health Works (Body Esteem)
www.womenshealthworks.org.au
Centre for Clinical Intervention (Eating Disorder Program)
www.cci.health.wa.gov.au

Victoria

Eating Disorders Victoria
www.eatingdisorders.org.au

Canada

National Eating Disorders Centre (NEDIC)
www.nedic.ca

Germany

Eating Disorders Network
www.netzwerk-essstoerungen.at

Hong Kong

Hong Kong Eating Disorders Association
www.heda-hk.org

Ireland

Bodywhys Eating Disorder Association of Ireland
www.bodywhys.ie

New Zealand

Eating Difficulties Education Network (EDEN)
www.eden.org.nz

United Kingdom

BEAT
www.b-eat.co.uk

USA

National Eating Disorders Association (NEDA)
www.nationaleatingdisorders.org
National Association of Anorexia Nervosa and Associated
Disorders, Inc (ANAD)
www.anad.org
Binge Eating Disorder Association (BEDA)
www.bedaonline.com

Lightning Source UK Ltd.
Milton Keynes UK
UKOW04f0802051017
310457UK00001B/44/P